A Teenager's (Absolutely Basic) Introduction to the New Testament

Jim Auer

LIGUORI
PUBLICATIONS

One Liguori Drive
Liguori, MO 63057-9999
(314) 464-2500

Imprimi Potest:
John F. Dowd, C.SS.R.
Provincial, St. Louis Province
The Redemptorists

Imprimatur:
+ Edward J. O'Donnell
Vicar General, Archdiocese of St. Louis

ISBN 0-89243-257-8
Library of Congress Catalog Card Number: 86-82167

Copyright © 1986, Liguori Publications
Printed in the United States of America

Table of Contents

1

Yes, You Have to Read This First

This chapter of a book is usually called the "Introduction." Notice how sneakily we avoided that word in the title. That's because some people have a really nasty habit of skipping Introductions.

Be honest: Haven't you often skipped right past an Introduction? Some folks even open books in the middle or toward the end and begin reading at that point. They figure if the author has something really important to say, he or she probably will work up to it gradually and put it in the middle of the book or almost at the end, so there's no sense wasting time on the small stuff in the beginning.

Read this Introduction.

Or the ghosts of the demon-infested swine recorded in Luke 8:32-33 will haunt your locker, your gym bag or purse, and your stereo radio cassette recorder.

I'm curious to know why you're reading this book. Since we're not likely to meet and discuss it, let's list the two most common possibilities.

1. School. You're taking a course on the New Testament. Your teacher has the knowledge and background of a professional Scripture scholar combined with the personality of a Marine drill sergeant. So you figure you'll have to know a lot more than the plots of the parables and miracle stories you remember from your grammar school religion classes. In other words, you could use a little help. OK, this book will give you a little help. Maybe more than a little.

But only if you give the whole ball game a fair shot!

This book is not like those summaries of great works of literature that some folks (but certainly not you or me!) consult in the library around 7:30 P.M. on the evening before the English test. These poor creatures sort of "forgot" to read *Julius Caesar,* and now it's not possible to wade through all that plot (and all that Old English prose) by 9:15 tomorrow morning. However, the reference section of the library has this really handy set of summaries of classic stuff. . . .

Don't do that with the New Testament. (Or *Julius Caesar,* for that matter. You'll miss a really good story.)

If you're supposed to read Mark, Romans, First Corinthians, and Revelation, *read them.* Don't forget (or "forget") about them until the evening before that great mystic ritual called a Religion Exam, and then try to skim through this book for some instant-yet-in-depth knowledge which you can scatter impressively across the pages of the exam. It won't work.

You probably have a textbook to go with the course, too. *Read it.* If it's hard to understand, read it again. Same way with the New Testament itself.

If you're watching a film on a VCR and you miss some dialogue, or you're not positive what the bad guy left behind at the scene of the crime, you press "Rewind" and re-watch that part, right? Your eyes and your brain have a "Rewind" button, too. Use it. Re-read anything you don't understand.

2. Gift. It's Christmas or your birthday or your graduation, or maybe your family exchanges gifts on Groundhog Day or something. Whatever the occasion, somebody thought a book on the New Testament would be just the perfect thing for you.

Maybe you're really glad about getting this book because you enjoy reading the Scriptures and you like to learn new things about them and understand them better. Or, at least you figure you always did intend to read the New Testament someday and this seems like a good time to start since somebody gave you a book about it. Terrific. We should have a good time together in these pages.

On the other hand, maybe you wanted the newest album by The Basement Slime but you got this book instead. So you politely said, "Oh, wow, Aunt Margaret . . . gee . . . thanks, this is really terrific," or some similar, tiny, little alteration of how you really felt.

Sorry about that. I know what it's like to get gifts you never wanted. But now that we're stuck with each other, let's make the best of it. More important, let's learn something about the New Testament.

You mean read it even if I don't *have to* for class?

Sure. Yes. Absolutely.

Now?

Well, if you're really pressed you could probably wait till next week.

Why?

This might be a great occasion for that classic remark, "Try it — you just might learn something." But that remark usually sounds like the speaker means, "I have little hope for your future; nevertheless, I'm fulfilling my responsibility toward you by pointing out an opportunity." I don't want to come across like that.

Trouble is, that remark does say what I want to say — but without the sarcasm. I do invite you to try it: *Read* the New Testament. No, not necessarily all of it straight through. Just get started on it. The chances are excellent that you will learn something. After all, you're not an idiot or an atheist. If you were, someone would not have given you this book. Moreover, there's a definite chance it'll be fun.

So you say, "That's what I'm afraid of. If I start reading the Bible a lot and like it, I might begin to be . . . you know. . . ."

Strange, right?

Right.

Forget it. If you're not strange now, you won't get that way from reading the New Testament. You might start thinking more deeply about your life and how you want to live it and how you want it to turn out. But that's not *strange*.

Whatever the reason for your having this book in your hands, I want you to know a couple things about it.

First, it's intended to be a very basic introduction to the study of the New Testament. That doesn't mean it's written for itty bitty munchkins. It simply means that this book assumes that you are not already a Scripture scholar, but someone wanting to learn the basic ideas necessary for understanding the New Testament. It explains basic things in a very basic manner.

So you may find yourself reading some items and thinking, "*I* knew that," or "I *sort of* knew that." Great. Enjoy the feeling.

And you may find yourself reading some items and thinking, "I get it now — I heard about that before but I didn't really understand it." In that case, we will have met with success.

Second, this book is intended to be at least moderately fun to read. This might disappoint or confuse some folks who feel that a really worthwhile book on Scripture should sound scholarly and pious.

Well, that's it. We made it through an entire Introduction. Thanks for hanging on. Now we can get started.

Incidentally, if your religion teacher does have a personality like a Marine drill sergeant, give him or her a big smile sometime for no reason at all. It might change things.

2

What's In the New Testament?

Twenty-seven books. Seems simple enough — but it's not. To begin with, they're not books in the way we use the word today. Hardly any of the twenty-seven documents is long enough to be a book. Several are so small they'd fit on a couple sides of looseleaf paper.

The "books" of the New Testament are arranged so that similar types of writing are grouped together. Here's a simple outline:

1. The Four Gospels: Matthew, Mark, Luke, John. In these four documents we find "The Jesus Story." Sometimes they're called biographies of Jesus, but that's not an accurate description of them. The Gospels feature a type of writing that was never used before and that hasn't been used since.

Matthew, Mark, and Luke are so similar in many ways that they're often grouped together and called the Synoptic Gospels. "Synoptic" is Greek for "one-eye" and implies that the three Gospels are so alike that the events they portray could have been viewed from a single perspective, or through the eye of one person.

The Gospel of John is very different in style and structure from the three Synoptic Gospels. More on all that later.

2. The Acts of the Apostles: There's only one document in this category — The Acts of the Apostles. The title is a little misleading. You won't find much material about the actual apostles or the actions they performed. Peter is the only one of the eleven original apostles who plays a significant role in Acts. The first part of Acts tells about some of the major events that happened to Peter and the Christian community in the first few years after Jesus returned to his Father. The second half of Acts tells about the journeys of Saint Paul.

3. Letters: (sometimes called "Epistles," an old-fashioned word for a formal letter). There are twenty-one of them and they can be divided into several categories:

Letters written by Paul or ascribed to Paul. ("Ascribed" means the letter-writer signed the name of Paul, even though Paul actually may not have composed and written the letter himself. More on that later.) Some of these letters were written to whole communities of people: Romans, First and Second Corinthians (Paul wrote them at least twice), Galatians, Ephesians, Philippians, Colossians, and First and Second Thessalonians. The names of these documents come from the places where Paul's audiences lived. If Paul were living today and wrote a letter to the Christians in, let's say Dayton, Ohio, there would be a Letter to the Daytonians. Other Pauline Letters were written to individual people: Titus, Philemon, and two to Timothy.

The Letter to the Hebrews. The author is not identified and to this day remains something of a mystery. It is quite clear, however, that the author was *not* Paul. For this and other reasons, this letter is in a class by itself.

The "Universal" Letters. These letters don't have a specific audience (like Romans or Timothy), so they're called "universal." They're ascribed to various apostles: James, First and Second Peter, First, Second, and Third John, and Jude.

4. The Book of Revelation: This is a document that seems very strange to us today. It uses a type of writing called "apocalyptic writing," which we generally do not use anymore. That makes it more difficult to understand. Even the smartest Scripture scholars can't quite figure out or agree on the meaning of some parts of the

Book of Revelation. But it makes interesting reading, and parts of it *are* very understandable. One thing is certain: Revelation does *not* predict twentieth-century earthquakes, wars, alien invasions, killer bees, or any similar jazz, in spite of what some people may try to tell you.

The New Testament writings are generally divided into chapters and verses. They weren't originally written that way, of course. The structure of chapters and verses was added much later to make it easier to locate and refer to specific parts. Otherwise, instead of simply saying, "Romans, chapter 13, verse 7," you'd have to say something like, "It's toward the end of the Letter to the Romans, but not right at the end; it's a little more than halfway between the middle and the end." It'd be a hassle without chapters and verses. Four New Testament Letters (the Letter to Philemon, the Second and Third Letters of John, and the Letter of Jude), however, are so short that their content is delineated only by verses and not chapters.

But after you get familiar with some of the New Testament documents, you may think that the folks who marked out the chapters and verses could have done a better job. In many cases you'd be right. The chapters don't always provide a logical outline for the ideas being presented. Some stories begin in one chapter and carry over into the next. Sometimes a single chapter contains many different themes or messages. But don't sweat the small stuff. Just be thankful that someone was wise enough to mark out the chapters and verses to help you find your place and locate particular passages.

Many editions of the New Testament have added headings in large or boldface type to form an outline of major sections or ideas. While these are not present in the original manuscript and thus are not part of the inspired text, they do help the reader to get a better picture of the material. Skimming over them before you begin reading the entire document will give you a brief "table of contents."

Some parts of the New Testament are more important or more interesting than others. This book and similar introductions to the New Testament can help people better understand the value and importance of the Scriptures.

The New Testament features a great variety of writing styles. The four Gospels intertwine parables, sayings of Jesus, miracle stories, healings, and several other distinct types of writing. The twenty-one Letters are also quite varied in terms of style and format. Some are pretty formal and logical, while others are newsy and folksy. The Acts of the Apostles uses many of the same writing styles as the Gospels, while the Book of Revelation has its own unique style.

You'll find a lot to like and a lot to learn in the New Testament.

3

Not All Bibles
Say the Same Thing

Jesus didn't speak English; he spoke Aramaic, which is a dialect of Hebrew. Paul didn't write his Letters in English either; he wrote in Greek. The only way we're going to find out what Jesus said and what Paul and the other New Testament authors wrote is by reading somebody's English translation of the original documents. OK, you knew that, right?

But there are some real problems in that seemingly simple situation. First of all, we don't *have* the original documents. They're not in a maximum security, glass-enclosed case in a museum somewhere.

What we have are copies, not originals — and not all the copies are 100% identical. Luckily, there aren't truckloads of major differences, but there are some. Since different translators have used different sources (copies), that's going to create some variations in their final results.

A more important reason for differences in biblical translations is the fact that there is no one single way to translate something from one language to another. Let's use a simple Latin sentence as an example: *Magna voce clamavit.*

We can translate that very literally and say in English, "He cried out with a great voice." It sounds kind of formal and rather nicely old-fashioned, doesn't it? But that's not the only possible way to translate it. We could also say, "He cried out in a very loud voice." That's accurate, but it's not very colorful.

Another possibility is: "He gave an ear-piercing scream." That gives a different sensation, doesn't it? It has more "punch" — but it also slyly adds something to the meaning: Now we get the impression that the cry came from pain or terror.

The possibilities go on and on. If we wanted a very informal translation, we could say, "He screamed like crazy." If we wanted a "down home" touch, we could say, "He hollered fit to bring the cows in from a mile off."

Which one is right? Well, they're all "right" in a way, but the best would be *the one which comes the very closest, using today's language, to what the original author meant and how he or she meant to say it.*

Now, when the author lived almost two thousand years ago in a culture very different from ours (and that's the case with the writers of the New Testament), we have a problem — or the translators have a problem. Actually, they have two problems: one is figuring out what the author meant to say, and the second is coming up with the best possible way to say that in English. (Pray for translators; they've got it tough.)

Let's look at several translations of Romans 6:1-2. The older translation that Catholics used for many years goes like this:

What are we to say? Shall we continue in sin that grace may abound? By no means! For how shall we who are dead to sin still live in it?

The translation most frequently used by Catholics today for the readings at Mass and for personal Scripture reading is called the *New American Bible*. It offers this translation of the verses in question:

What then are we to say? "Let us continue in sin that grace may abound?" Certainly not! How can we who die to sin go on living in it?

The *King James Version* (or *Authorized Version*) that Protestants used for years (and many still do) is similar; but notice the slight differences:

What shall we say then? Shall we continue in sin, that grace may abound? God forbid. How shall we, that are dead to sin, live any longer therein?

OK, let's bring on a much newer translation, the *New English Bible*.

What are we to say, then? Shall we persist in sin, so that there may be all the more grace? No, no! We died to sin: how can we live in it any longer?

Notice that the rather formal phrases "By no means" and "God forbid" have become "No, no!" in this translation. But the meaning is certainly the same in all four versions.

Now let's look at a translation that's *more* than a translation. The *New Testament in Modern English* might better be considered a paraphrase of the original text rather than simply a translation. It presents the following version of the verses in question:

Now what is our response to be? Shall we sin to our heart's content and see how far we can exploit the grace of God? What a ghastly thought! We, who have died to sin — how could we live in sin a moment longer?

"What a ghastly thought!" is obviously a mark of the *translator's* style, and not something present in the text or style of the original author. It would be similar to your translating that same phrase as "Oh, yuck!" That would be your particular language style, not the original's.

But more important, the phrase " . . . and see how far we can exploit the grace of God" is a definite attempt not just to translate but to *explain and interpret* the meaning.

Many people who are serious about studying Scripture object to this. They say that in such a version we're getting the translator's *opinion,* not just the words of Scripture. They're right! You would do well to avoid versions that are loose translations or which are actually labeled a "paraphrase."

Which translations are recommended depends on who's doing the recommending. Probably the most common translation used in

Catholic churches and schools is the *New American Bible*. It tries very hard to correspond closely with the vocabulary, style, and structure of the original text. The *Jerusalem Bible* offers a translation that is more conscious of the literary quality of the text. (For you *Lord of the Rings* fans, J. R. R. Tolkien was one of the advisors who was consulted about the literary style of the *Jerusalem Bible* translation.)

The *Good News Bible* (sometimes called *Today's English Version*) reads more like the modern English to which you are accustomed. If you use this translation, make sure that you have the ''Catholic'' edition with the complete Old Testament. Some Christian Churches do not accept all the books of the Old Testament that Catholics accept, so you want the edition which includes the ''Apocrypha.''

4

All This
New Scripture Stuff

A few years ago, a really unfortunate episode happened in a lot of schools and homes. (It still happens sometimes today, too.) It went like this.

The religion teacher would say something like, "Look, kids, that stuff about the Wise Men just isn't true. It makes a cute Christmas story and it sells plastic Wise Men statues, but it didn't happen like that."

Teachers who said that may have been sincere and thought that such announcements were necessary to bring religious education up-to-date. Maybe some of them just liked to shock people. Or maybe they wanted to appear cool and really with it. ("Sure, I'm religious and all, but, like, I'm *modern* about it, you know?")

In any case, the kids went home and casually mentioned to Mom and Dad that the Wise Men had had their series cancelled. Mom and Dad got severely bent out of shape, called the principal or pastor or both, and wrote a letter to the editor of the Catholic newspaper.

The teacher would respond by saying that some people were just too old-fashioned and couldn't understand "relevant" Scripture study. Mom and Dad would tell the kids that there were a lot of crackpots in the Church these days, even among so-called Scripture scholars, and the kids should not listen to Mr. or Ms. So-and-So anymore.

And the kids?

A lot of them figured that if adults couldn't agree on what

happened at Christmas, or what the Bible really meant, maybe this whole religion thing was just anybody's idea and you didn't have to take it very seriously after all.

Tragic. All caused by a lack of communication. Who's to blame? Don't look here for accusations. I enjoy an occasional risk, but don't expect me to point a finger of blame. I don't live that dangerously. Maybe part of it was and is nobody's fault; the confusion is part of the times in which we live. Maybe it's built into the present situation.

What situation? That's what this chapter is all about.

For a long time, people read the Bible as though it were the front page of the daily newspaper. (They did this even before there were newspapers.) They assumed that it was the same kind of writing: pure reporting.

Newspaper articles report the facts. They tell of things that occurred the way they're described — unless you're reading one of those national papers with stories like, "Giant Alien Mosquito Bites Arizona Housewife To Death!" If a newspaper story says there was a three car accident at the corner of Second and Elm at 5:37 P.M., we assume that it happened just that way: At exactly 5:37 P.M., three cars went crunch at Second and Elm.

But not all of the Bible is simple reporting. In fact, most of it is very different from newspaper reporting. So why did people think it was reporting? Mainly because there was no reason to think otherwise. The text of the Bible sounded like it was factually reporting history, so people figured it *was* reporting history.

"Besides," or so people believed, "this is the Bible, for heaven's sake! God himself is the Author. To say that even a tiny piece of it didn't mean exactly what it said . . . well, that would be calling God a liar, going against religion, and spitting in the face of everything good and holy. You'd have to be a demon to say such things!"

Consequently, the first modern Scripture scholars were considered demons.

Briefly, this is what happened. Beginning in the latter part of the nineteenth century, scholars began to learn much more about the times in which the Bible was written. Sciences like archeology and linguistics blossomed and provided better tools with which to study the past. Ancient cities were discovered and unearthed, giving scholars artworks, artifacts, historical data, and manuscripts to study. They began to understand ancient languages, civilizations, and cultures far better than they ever had before. In some ways, they began to *really* understand them for the first time.

These studies showed that people from past times and cultures were really different from us. It was more than just that they were born centuries before us. They were *really different* (that doesn't mean "weird," incidentally) *in the way they thought and in the way they communicated . . . including the way they wrote.*

Including the Bible.

Some of the ways they wrote, technically called "literary forms," aren't even used anymore. Now that's a real problem when we read them many centuries later. Unless we've been taught about the different literary forms used in the Bible, we do not recognize them and erroneously expect the words to mean what we would mean if we used them today. That can be misleading.

Let's say your health teacher puts up a poster which says, "Feel like a joint? Go ahead — fly! Get good and wasted — whaddya got to lose? Only your life . . . no big deal."

Now you have no problem understanding that. You know the poster isn't encouraging people to become professional druggies. The message, in fact, is exactly the opposite. That's because you're familiar with this kind of writing. You understand the literary form being used here: sarcastic satire.

But imagine the problems several centuries from now if people are unfamiliar with sarcastic satire . . . and somebody digs up this poster.

The Old Testament has more unfamiliar literary forms than the New Testament. The bottom line in both cases, however, is that we frequently need to understand how people thought and wrote *back then* in order to understand what the text of Scripture really means.

Noting that modern scriptural research began nearly one hundred years ago, you can see that it's taken a long time for the experts' findings to filter down to us regular old Scripture readers.

Some of the findings of scholars and researchers seem strange and make people uneasy. And that's stating it mildly! Have you ever heard someone say, ''They're trying to tear down the good old solid religion. Used to be, this was this and that was that, no questions asked. Now they say it's all symbols and that kind of stuff — I tell ya, I dunno what's gonna happen, but I don't like it. I still believe that whatever the Bible says, that's the way it is. The Church has changed too darn many things already, and I'm not going along with changing the Bible.''

OK. If you hear something like that, don't immediately tune out the speaker. Don't feel duty-bound to point out that he or she is hopelessly old-fashioned. Remember that it's very difficult for people to change their way of looking at something which they've loved and which has been important to them for a long time.

And don't tune yourself out at this point, either. This would be an easy place to decide, ''I'm not going to tie up part of my life studying a bunch of ancient cultural stuff just so I can have a decent shot at figuring out the Bible.''

If you've gotten that impression, let me correct it. You don't have to spend half your life studying ancient history, culture, and language just to squeeze a half ounce of understanding from a couple verses of Scripture. Not everything in the Bible is written in a mysterious literary form that takes a team of experts to interpret. A lot of the Bible, especially the New Testament, is very clear even to us in the twentieth century.

For example, when Paul tells the Colossians, ''Stop lying to one another'' (Colossians 3:9), you don't need a university full of Ph.D's to help you figure that out.

5

Inspiration: Does God Guarantee the Punctuation, Too?

Try to imagine this scene . . . CAMERA shows closeup of rough, masculine hands skillfully sewing a seam in a piece of heavy canvas. CAMERA backs to reveal a full-length shot of the man. We see that it is Saint Paul, pursuing his trade as a tentmaker. Suddenly there is a rumble from the sky overhead.

God (off camera): Paul? Paul!

Paul: Yes, Lord. Your servant waketh. I mean waiteth. Well, actually both.

God: Good. Put down your needle and get a stylus. I feel like writing today.

Paul: Your wish is my command, Lord. Who are you writing — sorry, *to whom* are you writing this time?

God: I think I'll do another letter to the Corinthians.

Paul: A sequel — terrific! Okay, I'm ready, but don't go too fast. You know how big my handwriting is, and I'm trying to write smaller so we can save on papyrus — so I have to write slowly.

God: No problem. Let's start like this: "Paul, by God's will an Apostle. . . ."

Well, that's one way of looking at "biblical inspiration." We usually use the word "inspiration" to indicate the way somebody got a terrific idea or devised a powerful example. That's not what inspiration means when we're talking about the Bible, however, even though the Bible is full of terrific ideas and powerful examples.

Biblical inspiration refers to the role or action of God in the formulation of the Bible. Not all Christians agree, however, about the exact role of God in this process.

Practically everybody agrees that God had *something* to do with the development of the Bible, but that doesn't say very much. Some large remaining questions are: "How did God arrange for the Bible to be written?" and "What's the bottom line — if God inspired the Bible, does that mean everything in it is absolutely true?"

Few people believe the process of inspiration to be like the script which began this chapter — God literally dictating words out loud to people like Paul, who simply acted as first-century stenographers. Most people would say, "God gave the biblical authors the *ideas* that he wanted to get across. Then they wrote in a style that was appropriate for their audience."

OK. But that's not an easy sentence either. For an example, let's go back to those three Wise Men — actually called astrologers in some modern biblical translations. Was their visit an idea that God put into Matthew's head? Was it an event that happened just as it is described in chapter two of Matthew's Gospel? Or were the Wise Men *Matthew's way* of getting across God's idea about Jesus reaching out to people of all nations? (Notice that the Gospels of Mark and John say nothing about Jesus' birth and that Luke's account differs slightly from Matthew's.)

Good question. Whole books have been written about the meaning of inspiration so we can't expect to define and explain this concept completely and for all time in just a few pages. Very briefly, the Catholic position on inspiration is this: Yes, the Bible was God's idea. He wanted to communicate with people through this special writing. He prompted certain people to write. And there were definite ideas he wanted to get across.

God gave the biblical authors the freedom to figure out the best ways to communicate those ideas. So what did they choose? Obviously, they selected ways that would work for the people to whom they were writing. They chose writing styles and formats that made sense to people of that particular time and place — the specific, original audience. Centuries later, we sometimes need a little help in recognizing and understanding those writing styles and images that are unfamiliar to us today.

What's *guaranteed* to be true in the Bible is the religious truth that God wants to communicate to us in order to bring us the good news of salvation that will help us arrive safely at the Great Racquetball Court in the Sky. (That's just my way of looking at it; I love racquetball.)

Here's that idea again in somewhat more official words. This is from the *Dogmatic Constitution on Divine Revelation,* a heavy but marvelous document which the bishops produced at the Second Vatican Council: "The books of Scripture must be acknowledged as teaching firmly, faithfully, and without error that truth which God wanted put into the sacred writings for the sake of our salvation"(#11).

Now there are quite a few people who don't accept this current position of the Catholic Church. They believe in the "literal inerrancy" of the Bible and in a "literal interpretation." ("Whatever it says, that's the way it is.")

So they're likely to see the Catholic position as watering down the Bible, as not taking it seriously, misreading it — and just plain *wrong.*

You may find this difficult to deal with, but don't argue about the Bible, OK? It was written to strengthen the faith of believers. It was never meant to be used in order to conquer opponents and prove how wrong they are. If a friend of yours is sincerely convinced of literal interpretation, don't blast him or her with, "Man, are you ever dumb! Haven't you heard about literary forms and all that stuff?"

Something like this would be a lot better: "I don't think we're going to agree on everything in the Bible, and I really don't want to hassle about it. But I think it's great that the Bible means so much to you. It means a lot to me, too, so at least we have that much in common."

And don't feel terribly superior, either. That other person might be doing a terrific job of living his or her Christian faith — and that *is* the bottom line. A person could *know* a lot about modern biblical studies and still be a Christian zero in daily life.

6

The Authors
of the New Testament

You may not be terribly concerned about precisely who wrote various sections of the New Testament.

Good thing, because for some sections we don't know the name of the exact author. Trying to determine the author of some documents has led experts down fascinating trails. These experts not only read ancient languages, they're able to detect differences in vocabulary and style in those languages, the way a modern authority on English literature could tell the writings of Ernest Hemingway from those of John Steinbeck. Despite all their knowledge, however, they can't always determine the exact and final author of a book or section of a book in the Bible.

You might wonder, then, why certain parts of the New Testament are credited to a particular person when scholars reject or question that person's authorship. For example, many experts believe that the author of the Gospel according to Matthew is unknown and was quite probably not the Apostle Matthew, the tax collector. Then why was he ever listed as the author?

There are several possibilities. One is that the early Christians considered it very important for a document about their faith to be "the real thing." One way of showing this would be to list as the author one of the original people who knew Jesus.

Here is another possible scenario: The document was named after a certain individual because it contained the teaching of this important person, although the actual writing and editing was done by someone else or even by several different people over a period of time. Finally, it's possible that a document was named in honor of one of those early, respected figures in the Christian community in the hope that more people would read it and believe its message to be authentic.

Here is a summary of New Testament authors, from certain to uncertain, based on recent scholarly opinion. Remember that this could change as more studies are done.

Author Certain:

The Gospel according to Luke and the Acts of the Apostles were written by Luke, a companion and fellow worker of Paul.

The Letters to the Romans, 1 and 2 Corinthians, Galatians, Philippians, 1 and 2 Thessalonians, and Philemon were written by Paul, the convert from Judaism.

Author Less Certain:

The Gospel according to Mark was quite possibly written by the individual named John-Mark. He is mentioned in Acts as being a companion of Peter.

The Gospel according to John was perhaps composed by a group of people who were very much influenced by the Apostle John.

The Letters to the Ephesians, Colossians, 1 and 2 Timothy, and Titus were traditionally associated with Paul. Now it appears more likely that his close associates and followers actually wrote these letters and signed Paul's name to make them seem more authentic.

The Letters of James, 1 and 2 Peter, 1, 2, and 3 John, and Jude were traditionally associated with the early Church leaders of those names. Their personal authorship is now being questioned.

The Book of Revelation may well have been written by a man named John, but probably not the Apostle John nor the person associated with the Gospel or the Letters of John.

Author Unknown:

The Gospel according to Matthew and the Letter to the Hebrews present the most difficulties. Scholars have come up with some interesting possibilities for these two, but there's no huge amount of evidence for any particular theory.

Does it make a difference who wrote what? To scholars, yes, for reasons that are a little too complicated to explain here. But for most people, no.

Do we lose faith in the Gospel of Matthew because it doesn't seem as though the Apostle Matthew wrote it? Are we tearing down the New Testament and our faith by admitting that Paul may not have directly written "Paul's" Letters to Timothy?

Of course not. We believe they're *inspired* and contain truths of the faith that God wants us to know and follow in our daily lives. If we believe that, it doesn't make a huge amount of difference whether "Matthew's" Gospel was written by a guy named Matthew or a guy named Mergatroyd.

As we'll find out in the next two chapters, none of the Gospel writers simply sat down and wrote a Gospel in the way an author does today. It was a rather complicated process, and many things went before the actual writing of the text that we have translated in our Bibles today.

In the meantime, however, our belief in inspiration does bring up another set of questions: "How do we know this or that book is really inspired? Who decided? how? and when?"

Good questions, because the twenty-seven pieces of the New Testament weren't the only writings about Jesus. During the first century after his death and Resurrection, many gospels, letters, and other documents were produced. Many of them, however, departed from what Christians accepted as the authentic teaching of Jesus.

About A.D. 140, a well-known teacher named Marcion was spreading ideas that Christians, in general, considered really off-the-wall. He also had his own list of sacred books. Among other things, Marcion said that only eleven Christian writings were real. Of the four Gospels, he accepted only part of Luke. He tossed out the entire Jewish Scriptures, or Old Testament!

The need for an officially accepted list of sacred books, both Jewish and Christian, became clear as time passed and confusion increased. Such a list was not formulated quickly or easily, however. For a long time there were lots of lists of accepted, rejected, and disputed books. Finally, a fourth-century bishop named Athanasius, working with other influential Church leaders, put together a list (called a "canon") of sacred books that almost everybody accepted. ("Canonical" means accepted as real or genuinely inspired.) Their list became the officially accepted list of books to be included in the Bible.

Here's what it took to be included in the list of official New Testament books.

1. The document was produced during the approximate life-span of the original apostles.

2. The teachings it contained were accepted by the Church as representing the true faith.

3. The writing was recognized and used throughout all areas where Christianity had spread.

The absolute, final "This is it" did not actually come until many centuries later. On April 8, 1546, the Council of Trent officially defined and proclaimed the list of twenty-seven New Testament books which we have today.

7

The Birth and Spread of the Gospels

The Gospels are the heart of the New Testament. We have four Gospels, four inspired documents that give us different word pictures of Jesus. While they are not identical, they each present the same "gospel" or "Good News," which is exactly what the word means.

Both the gospel (the style in which the message is written) and the Gospels (the four documents we have today) developed in stages.

It all started with Jesus himself. He proclaimed the good news of salvation and taught by word and by example. He died, rose from the dead, and returned to his Father. During this time, his close associates were attracted to him, amazed by him, confused and frustrated by him, and ultimately devoted to him.

No one was taking any notes, however, and tape recorders had not been invented yet.

Neither had duplicators, so Jesus didn't hand out purple worksheets and say, "Here, guys — work these exercises and answer the questions. This is all the stuff you gotta get straight so you can go out and preach to everybody when I leave."

Suddenly he was gone, and his friends were left with memories and a big job: To preach the Jesus story, the good news . . . the gospel.

They started simply, with just the very basics about Jesus and his saving death and Resurrection. You would probably start in the same way.

You might compare the experience of the apostles to this: After a long, difficult season, and a tense, complex but glorious final game, your team takes the state baseball or softball championship. You're delivering the news to somebody who hasn't heard it yet. What are your first words?

"Well, it all began back in early spring, at the very first team meeting when. . . . " Of course not.

"WE WON! WE TOOK STATE!! EVANS HOMERED WITH TWO ON IN THE BOTTOM OF THE NINTH — WE'RE NUMBER ONE!"

That's more like it.

And that's more like the way it was with the apostles, too. The first preaching and writing presented the absolute basics of the good news. It's something called the "core message" or *kerygma* (a Greek word meaning "announcement" or "proclamation"). We'll find that core message in several places in Acts. (Read Acts 3:11-21 and 4:8-12.)

Jesus came, sent by God. He died — but he rose again and he's Lord. We witnessed this. We're telling you so you can believe — because if you believe in Jesus you can be saved from your sins!

In its absolutely simplest form, that's the gospel.

As you might expect, listeners wanted to know more. "What else did he do?" "What were some of the things he taught?" "Where did he come from?" "Did he ever say anything about. . . . ?"

The apostles had to piece together as much as they could remember about things Jesus did and said. They had to recall things which, at the time, they never counted on needing to remember. As you might expect, different people remembered different things — and sometimes they disagreed on minor details or the exact words used by Jesus in a particular situation.

Collections of "Jesus stories" grew. They contained some "sayings" or teachings of Jesus, including the parables he told. Other people recalled and compiled accounts of the miracle stories and healing stories. Still others focused on the events of Jesus' death and Resurrection, noting that these were the key events in the process of salvation. For many years these collections were the sources of information about Jesus.

As time went on, believers decided, "We'd better write these things down before they get lost." So written collections appeared. Exactly how many there were is uncertain. None of these first written collections of stories and sayings has survived, but scholars draw an almost certain conclusion that they existed and were used in the four Gospels which we accept today. More on that shortly.

It was Mark who made the leap from these earlier, simpler writings to actually writing a gospel. You might say that he invented the gospel as a style of writing.

A gospel isn't a biography, certainly not as we know it. Biography is heavy on getting times and places and the order of events straight. The Gospels are not primarily concerned with historical accuracy.

If you write a paper about the life of Abraham Lincoln, and your history teacher says, "Your paper gives some great insights into Lincoln and what his life meant — but your sense of historical facts and details is pretty sloppy," then you may have written something a bit like a gospel.

Now don't get the idea that the Gospel writers were deliberately careless or sloppy about the facts of history. That's just not the kind of writing they were doing. They weren't into historical, biographical details. They were writing . . . well, gospels, and that's a different thing.

For example, the great collection of teachings in Matthew's Gospel known as the "Sermon on the Mount" (chapters 5-7) describes Jesus as teaching from a mountainside. Luke has Jesus standing on flat ground. Matthew lists eight beatitudes; Luke has four; the Gospels of Mark and John do not even record this event from Jesus' life.

If you're hyper about history (as we understand it today), you'll say, "Wait a minute — can't those guys get it straight? Where did this happen — on a mountain or on flat ground?"

Wrong kind of question when you're reading a gospel.

Matthew's mountain is there for a reason. He was writing for Jewish Christians. Mountains were strong symbols to those people. A mountain was a place where God communicated with his people, where people received messages from the Lord. By placing Jesus on a mountainside when he proclaimed the New Testament "law," the writer of Matthew's Gospel linked Jesus to Moses, who received the Old Testament "law" (The Ten Commandments) on Mount Sinai.

Why does Matthew put this great collection of Jesus' teachings on a mountain? It's his way of saying, "This is straight from the Lord. This is important and official. This shows that Jesus is an important person." And his original audience understood that perfectly. They didn't get hung up on things like, "Well, how high was this mountain?" and "How could the people toward the bottom hear what Jesus was saying when there was no loudspeaker system?"

Luke's audience didn't have a Jewish background. For them, mountains were things that made travel a hassle, not religious symbols. Luke doesn't bother putting a mountain in his collection of Jesus' teachings.

Several phrases have been used to describe the gospel style of writing. "Faith-history" and "faith-portrait" are two ways of saying that the authors gave a story of faith rather than a precise historical account of events. Now the writers didn't merely spin events out of their imaginations — don't think that the Gospels are "stories made up to get a point across but that didn't actually happen." That's not the case at all. It's just that the whole theme and purpose of each Gospel is to convey the meaning of Jesus' life, death, and Resurrection for our lives.

To get across that theme, the Gospel writers (they're often called "evangelists") began with some historical events — things Jesus said and did. Each writer selected events that would be especially significant for his particular audience. Then he arranged and related those events *in a way that would convey that theme* — the meaning of the risen Jesus in one's life — to his particular audience.

The Gospels weren't written to convince non-believers to believe in Jesus. It's not likely that a Roman who believed in Jupiter would have read one of them and said, "Wow, this proves beyond any doubt — Jesus is the one to follow."

The Gospels were written to provide insights into the life and teachings of Jesus and to strengthen the faith of people who already believed that he was the risen Lord. Anyone who reads the Gospels looking for airtight arguments and inescapable proofs about Jesus will end up unsatisfied.

In the Gospels we have a unique mixture of ordinary history (the kind we're used to) and writing that would *not* qualify as the kind of history we write today. Sometimes they're side by side.

A great example of this is found in the Gospels of Matthew, Mark, and Luke as they relate the events surrounding the moment of Jesus' death on the Cross. In each case, one verse says that Jesus died and the other verse says that at the same moment the curtain in the sanctuary was torn in two from top to bottom. (Read Mark 15:37-38; Matthew 27:50-51; Luke 23:45-46.)

Jesus' death is absolutely historical, even by our "get the facts completely straight" view of history. This is one time when the Gospels accurately record an actual historical event. We have records of his death from documents outside of the New Testament.

What about the splitting of the sanctuary curtain?

That curtain separated the Holy of Holies, the most sacred place in the temple, from the rest of the temple. Only the high priest was allowed to enter the Holy of Holies, and he could enter it only once each year, on the Day of Atonement. He brought burnt offerings, animals who had been sacrificed. The blood of the animals was applied inside the Holy of Holies, the closest place to the very presence of God, as a way of atoning or "making up for" sins.

Do you start to see a connection? The Gospels are trying to draw a parallel between the Good Friday sacrificial death of Jesus on the Cross and the Old Testament animal sacrifice on the Day of Atonement.

This verse is saying that the death of Jesus and the shedding of his blood is our new offering for sin. And the splitting in two of the curtain is saying that the old way — bringing animal sacrifices to the Holy of Holies — has ended. Instead of an annual animal sacrifice that really didn't make up for sins, Jesus has made up for our sins once and for all by shedding his blood on the Cross.

Those two verses make a great example of that special blend or style of writing we call a gospel. They show how we can understand the Gospels if we know something about how they were written and the audience for whom they were first written.

Don't panic! You don't have to spend twenty years at Harvard getting Ph.D's in Hebrew, Greek, and Roman culture in order to "get something out of" reading the Gospels. Simply reading, studying, thinking, and reflecting can help you begin to understand the meaning of the Scriptures.

8

Helpful Hints for Understanding the Gospels

Remember a few pages ago when I promised to provide further information about those early written collections of sayings and stories that came before the Gospels? This is the time. It will also help if you recall what was said earlier about the striking similarities in the Gospels of Mark, Matthew, and Luke. Remember that they are called the "Synoptic Gospels." "Synoptic" is a Greek word meaning something like "similar outlook" or "seen through a single eye."

Pretend you're an English teacher. Three of your students are doing a writing assignment. They're all writing on the same topic at the same time. One student is in the classroom, one is in the library, and one is in the audiovisual room.

They turn in compositions which are astoundingly similar. True, the compositions were all supposed to be on the same topic, but the similarity goes way beyond that. The three papers have many actual sentences and paragraphs that are very similar — sometimes almost identical. Yet the students wrote separately.

The detective work here isn't too difficult. There must have been another paper, one written before the three students began theirs. Each of the three students must have had a copy of it before writing his or her paper.

Something like that happens when we study Matthew, Mark, and Luke closely. Most of the material in Mark also appears in

Matthew. The details in Luke are similar to those reported in Mark and Matthew but not always identical. The structure and outline of events in all three are quite similar.

Experts guessed that there was a common source, a document no longer in existence, which all three drew from, somewhat as the three students did in our example. It contained a collection of sayings attributed to Jesus. This document is called Q, the first letter of "Quelle," the German word for "source."

That's a *simple* version of how the three Synoptic Gospel writers had a common source. It's super simple. There are several variations on this basic idea. You can find them by checking other books on the New Testament. Often they're illustrated by means of diagrams with arrows all over the place, going to and from the Synoptic Gospels and various earlier sources.

For example, not everybody agrees that Mark's Gospel (the first one that was written) used Q. Some think he had other sources, but not Q. Most agree that the writers of Matthew and Luke used the Gospel of Mark *and* Q. Some think that the writers of Matthew and Luke each had other written sources available to him alone. These have been labeled M and L. Still others say there was a "triple tradition" (in addition to Q) that all three used.

If at this point you're thinking something like "AAAGHHH!", you can be forgiven. It's not easy to keep all this straight. And you don't have to keep it straight in order to profit from reading the Gospels.

But don't put it down as being totally stupid. ("Who cares about that stuff? Only eggheads.") Many of the things which help us understand the Gospels better are the results of complicated studies like these.

This particular kind, incidentally, is called "source criticism." This doesn't mean that experts don't like or are critical of the sources. "Criticism" here means a careful study of something.

This is not the only type of criticism that needs to be considered. There's more.

If you read more books about the New Testament, you'll hear about something called "form criticism." Again remember that "criticism" means the careful study of something. Let's use an example to illustrate form criticism.

You're talking to a group of young children about a person named Mr. Davis. These kids admire Mr. Davis very much since he did some things that profoundly influenced their lives. Let's say he began a school which has enabled them to succeed in a way they never dreamed they could. But Mr. Davis isn't there with them. He's either died or he's gone on to a different position.

Let's further say you know that Mr. Davis was extremely opposed to smoking. You know this for certain. Among other things, he had written a very strong, anti-smoking article for a national science magazine.

You want to make this point clear to them and get across Mr. Davis's ideas. But you also want to do it in a persuasive, entertaining way — a way that will really hit your audience and have the effect Mr. Davis himself would want if he were there.

You decide that a familiar "Once upon a time, there was . . ." story will get his message across to these young kids. So you tell them this story: "A group of children just like you were gathered around Mr. Davis one day after school. They were sitting on the steps of the school listening to him talk, and he told this story: 'Once upon a time, there was a boy whose friend offered him a cigarette. . . . ' "

What's happening here? You're taking what you know to be Mr. Davis's ideas and message, and you're putting them in a form that's well-known to your audience, a form that will work well in getting that message across to them.

That's a simple example of what many scholars believe the Gospel writers did in writing down some accounts of what Jesus said and did. Remember their situation: They hadn't just talked with Jesus yesterday, or even last week or last year. Nobody had written down Jesus' talks, and nobody remembered them word for word. But they did know the basic ideas of his message. And they needed to communicate that message in a way that people would find interesting. So they used popular literary forms (stories, parables, dialogues, sayings) to convey Jesus' basic message of salvation.

Some people get anywhere from mildly surprised to violently bent out of shape at the idea that the Gospels may not contain, after all, the exact words of Jesus as he spoke them on some afternoon in Galilee. They point out that Jesus' words and ideas as recalled and related in the New Testament cannot be proven to be absolutely authentic, for example, in the way we can prove that John Kennedy really did deliver his famous Inaugural Address exactly as it is recorded. And they're correct in that.

Others feel a bit relieved because this view of how the Gospels were put together answers a nagging question: How did all those exact words get accurately preserved without the use of a tape recorder, or at least a professional scribe who knew shorthand?

There's a final type of study used by New Testament scholars. This is a process called "redaction criticism." *Hang on. This is the last of the heavy stuff for a while.*

Let's go back to the situation of Mr. Davis that we used before and the "Once upon a time" story, which showed a literary form at work. Now you're also going to be a *redactor*. This means you're something like an editor, and you have a special viewpoint in mind when you tell that story — and the viewpoint fits what your audience needs to hear and understand.

Let's say you believe very strongly in the need for independent thinking and not giving in to peer pressure. This isn't just your own idea, though. Independent thinking was another value that Mr. Davis considered important. His life was an example of independent thinking. Moreover, many of the children in your present audience are extremely influenced by peer pressure. Some of them are starting to smoke just to look cool in front of their Joe Cool friends.

Now your version of the story might go like this: "A group of children just like you were gathered around Mr. Davis one day after school. They were sitting on the steps out front listening to him talk, and he told them this story: 'Once upon a time, there was a boy whose friend offered him a cigarette and told him he had to smoke it in order to be cool. The boy didn't really want the cigarette. But he felt he didn't have many friends, so he wanted to be part of the cool crowd because they seemed popular.' "

That's a *redaction:* applying your slant or coloring to a story when the situation seems to need it — and when that slant or coloring is in tune with the ideas of the person you're talking about.

Again, some people get anywhere from surprised to freaked out at the suggestion that this may have taken place in the texts we now know as the four Gospels.

In trying to understand the Bible and the explanations offered for its composition, you have to steer a course between two opposites. One is just accepting anybody's brand new theory about something in Scripture. Be careful if you hear somebody say, "I read an article that said the part in the Bible where whatchamacallit happened doesn't actually mean such-and-such at all — this article said that the Bible only says that because of this-'n-that-and-so-forth, and actually all it really means is. . . . "

Check it out, certainly before you re-design your life around any brand new interpretation that somebody is supposed to have recently developed.

The other opposite to avoid is being suspicious of anything new or different, of everything that isn't exactly "the way they used to teach it." We believe that Scripture is inspired, right? This means it has a message God wants us to hear so that we can be saved.

Now if somebody discovers things about Scripture that open up a better understanding of what it really intended to say in the first place, then we should be glad that we're better able to learn what God wants us to learn.

If new insights into Scripture change what I *thought* it meant and I'm upset over it, well, that's life. On the other hand, refusing to be open is like telling God, "Listen, I like *my* version of your message better than *your* version." That's a little arrogant.

9

Some Groups That Are Real Characters

If you look at the Gospels as a story, you'll find that some of the characters in the story are *groups* of people rather than individuals. Some, such as the Pharisees, are mentioned rather often; others less so. In this chapter we'll look at some of the groups mentioned in the Gospels.

The Jews

The New Testament often refers simply to "the Jews." You know that's a very big group. In New Testament times, Jews lived both in the original homeland of Palestine and outside it, in cities throughout the Mediterranean world. The Jews who lived outside Palestine are sometimes called Jews of the "Diaspora," which means "scattering." There was even a sizeable community of Jews in Rome itself.

These Jews who lived outside Palestine are also sometimes called Hellenists, which does not mean hellraisers. (Some Jews *in* Palestine tended to be that.) It comes from the Greek word for "Greek." Living outside Palestine, the Hellenist Jews became quite familiar with Greek education and culture, and even abandoned some of their Jewish heritage and customs. We would say they were more "with it" in terms of the big world out there. (That doesn't always mean better.)

But when the New Testament uses the term "Jews," it seldom

means all Jews everywhere. Often it means a small group in a particular place who didn't represent all Jews everywhere. Sometimes it seems to refer mainly to the more prominent members or influential leaders of the Jewish community in a particular place. When John's Gospel tells us that the apostles had locked the doors "for fear of the Jews" after the death of Jesus, it certainly wasn't the entire Jewish nation they were afraid of. It was more likely the leaders who had engineered Jesus' arrest and crucifixion.

The Pharisees

In the Gospels, especially Matthew, the Pharisees often come across as bad guys. Jesus is seldom portrayed using harsh language or publicly criticizing people; whenever he does so, his targets are almost always the Pharisees. (And the Scribes. We'll get to them in a moment.)

This might seem strange when you realize that the Pharisees were a group of Jews that tried to take their religion seriously. They really wanted to be holy. Yet they came across as phonies. We even have the English words "pharisaic" and "pharisaical," which mean acting like a hypocrite . . . pretending to be something you're not.

Why?

Their view of religion equaled "Law," pure and simple. In their view, holiness meant observing all the details of the Jewish law (the law of Moses) — plus many extra details which they had added. They had over 600 individual laws governing all aspects of religious practice as well as events of everyday life. They had laws governing eating, drinking, washing, and just about everything else you might consider. Religion for them had become a matter of performing all the correct actions.

They were apparently sincere in this — they really thought that doing all these things would make them holy. Observing the Pharisees, it became clear that many of them felt superior to the "ordinary" folks who didn't take all these laws and rituals as seriously.

Jesus taught that simply performing certain actions and following certain rules isn't what religion is all about. He explained to the Pharisees that external actions have no meaning unless they have the love of God and neighbor in their hearts. The Gospels highlight Jesus' difficulties with the Pharisees by presenting some colorful confrontations between Jesus and the Pharisees.

Some of the Pharisees wanted Jesus out of the way. He was making them look bad. But they weren't all opposed to him; some checked out his teaching, accepted his message, and changed their outlook.

There's another reason why the Gospels, especially Matthew's, are so rough on the Pharisees. A four-year Jewish revolt against Rome (not a very smart move from a military standpoint) was crushed in the year 70. The temple was destroyed, Jerusalem was ruined, and thousands of Jews were killed. Many others were carried off into slavery. It looked as though the Jewish faith might practically disappear.

A group of Pharisees held a big meeting to make sure that wouldn't happen. They succeeded. They re-organized and streamlined the Jewish faith, so to speak — but along their lines. Part of that included a very official rejection of anything relating to this new Christian way of life. It was a way of telling Christians, "You are definitely the opposition." The author of Matthew's Gospel seems to be reacting somewhat to *these* Pharisees, not just the ones Jesus himself confronted. (Remember what we said before about redaction and how the writer and editor used the words and ideas of Jesus to address the problems of their own day.)

The Sadducees

The Sadducees are often linked with the Pharisees in opposing Jesus, yet they didn't believe the same things about their own

Jewish faith as most of the other Jews — especially the Pharisees. Opposition to Jesus may have been about all these two groups had in common. The Sadducees represented the high social class. In order to keep this position, they deliberately got along well with the Romans. (Some folks would call this "selling out.") At the time of Jesus, members of the Sadducee party served as priests of the temple, and the Romans nominated one of them to be the High Priest. When the New Testament mentions "elders," they seem to have been Sadducees.

The Zealots

Today we might call them "freedom fighters." None of the Jews liked being ruled by Rome, but this group of people positively couldn't stand it. They frequently plotted and schemed to throw off the Roman rule because they found it to be so oppressive and restrictive. They were responsible for the final revolt that ended in disaster in A.D. 70.

While very few Jews were actively involved in actual Zealot activities, many Jews were influenced by the Zealots' hope for a political Messiah — one who would make the Jews an independent nation again. One of Jesus' Apostles, Simon, was or had been a member of the Zealot party. (Don't confuse Simon the Zealot with Simon Peter, the most important Apostle.)

The Scribes

Scribes were the official intellectuals, the brain trust of the Jewish religion. Today we might call them theologians. It took many years of study to become a Scribe. Men were usually at least forty years old when they became recognized as Scribes. They held a respected position in the Jewish community. Scribes weren't necessarily members of any other particular group, but most of them were also Pharisees. A few were temple priests.

They gave a very strict interpretation of the law and added many additional prescriptions to the law.

The Publicans

Publicans were scum in the eyes of most Jews. The hatred is pretty understandable. Imagine our country being conquered and ruled by another, and one of your neighbors going to work for the invaders . . . and then collecting a healthy chunk of *your* paycheck to give to them! Chances are you're not going to feel terribly friendly toward that person.

Publicans were employed by the Romans to collect taxes from the Jews. That was bad enough, but on top of it some of them apparently collected a bit more than was actually due. Needless to say, they did not pass this extra on to the Romans but kept it for themselves.

The Samaritans

Samaritans were also scum to most Jews, but for different reasons. Their history before the time we meet them in the Gospels is complicated. The Samaritans of New Testament times had a mixed ancestry. Their forebearers were Jewish people who had intermingled with other races. Jews saw them as "halfbreeds." The Samaritans had their own version of the Jewish faith (although it may not have been drastically different from the faith of full-blooded Jews) and their own temple — still more reasons why the ordinary Jews did not get along with them.

Their district, Samaria, was between the districts of Galilee and Judea, where "real" Jews lived. Galilee lay to the north, Judea to the south. Traveling through Samaria from Galilee to Judea or vice versa could get very tense.

So, when Jesus showed an open, accepting attitude toward Samaritans, it was nothing less than shocking. Today we hear the

"Good Samaritan" parable and the ending seems almost logical. Because of the parable, the word "Samaritan" has overtones of "good guy." In New Testament times, however, the idea of a Samaritan being the good guy was a bombshell.

The Essenes

These people aren't actually characters in the Gospel, but many studies of the New Testament take note of them. They were a religious group of Jews who lived somewhat like monks on the western shore of the Dead Sea. There's a certain similarity of ideas and style in their writings and the New Testament writings attributed to John.

It's almost certain that the Essenes produced what are now known as the "Dead Sea Scrolls" or the "Qumran Scrolls," which were discovered in 1947 and have been extremely valuable to scholars. These scrolls provided scholars with very old copies of the Hebrew Scriptures, the Old Testament.

The Essenes believed that 'the end of time" was fast approaching and they prepared to meet their God by living holy lives. Ironically, that was the correct approach for them. Their community was destroyed when the Romans wiped out the rebellion in A.D. 70.

10

The All-Time
Great Preaching Tentmaker

One of the things you'll certainly want to do when you make it to that Great Study Hall in the Sky (OK, I'm sorry — that's a rotten description of heaven) is meet Paul. What a personality!

He wrote more individual pieces of the New Testament than anyone else. Some people have said that without Paul there wouldn't be a New Testament as we know it. Others have said that Paul was second only to Jesus himself in spreading the message of Christianity. We don't know everything about him, but what we do know is fascinating.

Paul was an *extremely* unlikely choice to spread the Christian message, but that's God for you. God doesn't always make *logical* choices; some of them are positively off the wall. (Funny, though — they always seem to turn out OK.)

Paul was born several years after Jesus. His parents were Jewish, but they lived outside Palestine in the city of Tarsus, not far from the northeastern coast of the Mediterranean Sea. Tarsus, a large city by the standards of that time, was the capital of a district called Silicia.

It was part of conquered territory (practically everything around the Mediterranean Sea was Roman-conquered territory). The Roman General who governed the area, Marc Antony, had made the city a "free city," so its citizens were Roman citizens. Being a

Roman citizen carried valuable legal privileges, which Paul later used to his advantage when he faced persecution as a Christian.

Remember the group of characters known as the Pharisees? Paul came to Jerusalem as a young man to study his faith under one of the master Pharisees. Paul himself became a super, high-tech Pharisee — a Pharisee plus. Following all the details and observing the finest interpretations of the law was extremely important to Paul. He guarded the truth of the law with a passion.

When someone or something seemed to attack that truth, Paul wanted to strike back and wipe out the error. For quite a while he thought that belief in Jesus was the error that needed wiping out.

That's what put him on the road to Damascus that fateful day. He was on his way to arrest Christians. Somewhere along that road one of the most stunning reversals in history took place. He encountered Jesus. The incident is described quite vividly in the Acts of the Apostles. (Read Acts 9:1-30 for the story of Paul's conversion, and the remainder of the book of Acts for a summary of Paul's early missionary activities.)

Very shortly after his encounter with the Lord, Paul became a believer in Jesus, a member of the very Christian community he had tried to destroy.

But his career as a fired up, never-say-die missionary didn't begin right after his conversion or even shortly thereafter. He spent some time, perhaps three years, in Arabia. It seems to have been a time of deep thinking. (You'd have a lot to sort out, too, if your life and beliefs had been turned upside down.)

He returned to Damascus and began preaching there. No doubt he was full of enthusiasm for the new faith, which was now quite clear in his mind. Imagine the hope and enthusiasm he put into that first preaching.

The results were amazing but probably not what Paul expected. His preaching caused full-scale riots. It got so bad that, to escape from Damascus alive, he had to be taken out of the city at night through an opening in the city wall.

Not exactly a successful beginning for the most famous apostle of the Christian faith.

Many of Paul's Jewish brethren saw him as a great renegade: a former champion of "our side" who had disgracefully defected to "their side." Paul would live amid this Jewish hostility for the rest of his life.

He seems to have gone to Jerusalem to meet Peter and James shortly after his preaching debut in Damascus. But he wasn't welcomed very warmly by them or by other Christians. Followers of Jesus had a tough time accepting Paul. After all, this was the fellow who had done everything he could to wipe them out not so long ago. After his cool reception by the Christian community, he returned to his home city of Tarsus, probably very discouraged, to sort things out still further.

He was "rescued" by Barnabas, a man of prestige among the Jerusalem Christians. Barnabas finally persuaded them to accept Paul. This acceptance by the very people Paul so passionately wanted to join had taken years.

The Christian community in Antioch (north of Jerusalem) appointed Paul and Barnabas to bring the gospel to lands where it had never been preached. With that, Paul began the missionary career that brought him great fame. He undertook three major journeys throughout the Mediterranean world to spread the good news.

It wasn't all fun. (Check out 2 Corinthians 11:24-27.) Throughout his missionary travels, Paul was strengthened by his love of Jesus and supported by the love he received from his "children," the converts he made. He regularly became involved in their problems, particularly their spiritual problems. He wrestled with their questions of faith. If they strayed from the Christian message he had preached to them, he was deeply hurt. While he felt personally betrayed, he was primarily upset that they were turning their backs on the truth which could save them.

He was very direct in his dealings with everyone. People always knew what Paul was thinking and where he stood. In his Letter to the Galatians, within a few paragraphs he compliments them on some things and criticizes them about others. He meant both intensely. (Read Galatians 1:1-10; 3:1-9.)

Like most people, he preferred peace and harmony but he wasn't afraid of tense confrontations where truth was at stake. On one occasion, the "opponent" he confronted was none other than Peter himself. (Read Acts 15:1-29 and Galatians 2:1-14 for two accounts of this controversy between Peter and Paul.)

All of this helped Paul to grow in his own understanding of the faith. People who study Paul's Letters, from his earliest ones to the ones he wrote at the end of his life, can see how he developed in his understanding of what it meant to be a Christian, a member of the living body of Christ on earth.

His Christian "career" began with a dramatic encounter. His wisdom and insights into the Christian life, however, didn't come to him in a package deal along with that conversion experience on the road to Damascus. He had to work at it — just like the rest of us.

11

Those First
Christian Folks

A very accurate subtitle for this chapter would be: *The hassles of being an early Christian.*

We can better appreciate the Gospels and understand the New Testament by studying the tremendous impact of Jesus' message on its first audience. While it's tough being a real Christian in the twentieth century, it wasn't a piece of cake in the first century either.

Sometimes we get an incorrect picture of Jesus' first followers. Books and articles and sermons can give the idea that the early believers understood what Jesus was all about from the time the Christian ball game first started. We can imagine that they loved each other to pieces, traveled around with "Honk If You Love Jesus" stickers pasted on the tail ends of their donkeys, and just generally floated around the Middle East on a terrific religious high.

Not quite.

Accepting Jesus wasn't always easy. Then, if you overcame your initial problems with his message and accepted him, your problems were often just beginning.

It's incredible that Christianity survived its infancy.

Imagine for a moment that a couple of your friends excitedly tell you that they've been in contact with a visitor from another galaxy. (Even wilder — imagine that a total stranger tells you this!) They claim to have received knowledge that was unknown until now and they want to share it with you.

This new information requires you to change much or all of what you've always believed. You're asked to revise many or most of your ideas about God. You're asked to change your political views. You're asked to turn many of your beliefs about what's important in life upside down.

That's a capsule of what it was like for many people to hear the Christian message when it was first delivered. Two very different types of people heard the message: Jews and Gentiles. Each had special problems understanding and accepting it.

To better understand the Jewish position, imagine this perspective. As you live your life, you probably hope for a time when things will be better. This doesn't mean everything is necessarily the pits right now. But you look forward to a future time when just about everything will be the way you want it and the way it's supposed to be.

The Jews did that, too. Their hope for the future was called "Messianism." It's an awfully complex idea, but in the simplest terms it meant that they awaited a time when their nation would be in great shape, when the rule of God would extend over the world, when people would be holy, and when everything would be cool.

A special person, a Messiah, was to come and bring about or at least begin this great situation.

In the meantime, the Jews waited and endured the problems and disappointments of life. They were especially upset by those rotten Romans. Romans — pagans with disgusting, false gods for heaven's sake — had conquered the Jewish homeland, Palestine, and were running the political show.

When he came, the Messiah definitely would do something about this.

Many Jews expected the Messiah to be a warrior or political revolutionary who would gather forces, kick the Romans out, let them know that Jupiter wasn't worth the papyrus his name was written on, and make things religiously and politically glorious for the Jewish people.

While this was the prevailing opinion, not all Jews had this vision of the Messiah. Some expected a more spiritual Messiah and looked for him to be a teacher of wisdom and a bringer of holiness. Others sincerely wanted and expected both a spiritual and political Messiah.

In any case, it's safe to say that most Jews expected some definite, observable difference in their world — a difference for the better — with the coming of the Messiah.

Jesus came and on the surface nothing seemed to change. Romans still ruled Palestine. In fact, Jesus was executed under Roman authority, and afterward things still seemed to stay about the same.

This was the Messiah? After hundreds of years of waiting, the Messiah comes as a carpenter's son, preaches for a rather short time, and then is executed under pagan authority?

You can imagine the understandable difficulty which many Jews experienced in hearing the Jesus-is-the-Messiah message for the first time. This Jesus was not the type of Messiah they wanted. He seemed to be powerless in both the political and the spiritual realm.

"Messiah," by the way, is a Hebrew word which means "anointed one." In Jewish history, people were anointed with oil when they were chosen for a special role or purpose in God's plan. The most important Anointed One, "The Messiah," was Jesus, the one whom God chose and sent to straighten everything out.

When you translate "Messiah" into Greek, you get "kristos." In English that becomes "Christ." So, "Jesus Christ" is not a first and last name like "Bob Smith." It means "Jesus the Anointed One." This is why Jesus is often referred to as "The Christ." Of course, only the followers of Jesus saw him as the Christ, the long-awaited Messiah. Others saw him as a trouble-maker, a sorcerer, or someone who should be persecuted.

Accepting Jesus and his message was just as difficult for the Gentiles, only for different reasons. "Gentiles," by the way, simply meant people who were not Jews — Romans, Greeks, Egyptians, you name it.

To accept the Christian message, Gentiles had to discard practically everything they believed about religion. Suddenly Jupiter and Venus, for example, were powerless nobodies — they didn't even exist. Instead, there was this *one,* invisible God who was everybody's *Father,* and who had chosen to communicate with people through his son.

This son was a member of a conquered nation. He worked as a carpenter most of his life. For a brief time he traveled around a relatively small area telling people to reform their lives and love one another. He was executed at the demand of some of his own people . . . but then he was raised to new life.

Wild.

To the Romans, this violated all their ideas of glorious power and control. To the Greeks, it violated all their ideas of logic and rational thinking. The Jews and Gentiles had other difficulties with Jesus and his ministry. By human standards, this message should not have been accepted, but it was accepted enthusiastically by many Jews and Gentiles.

That brings us to the first big Christian hassle.

The promise of the Messiah, remember, had been made to the Jews. In spite of being conquered politically, Jews generally considered themselves the most special folks on earth because God had communicated with them and had helped them throughout their history. They knew they had the right idea of God (one God . . . Yahweh . . . spiritual, invisible, almighty). Romans and such other critters might be militarily awesome, but they were quite confused when it came to religion. Besides, the Messiah was coming to fix things up and would those pagan folks ever be sorry then!

God had tried to tell the Jews, "Look, you're special to me, but I don't *hate* those other people. I want them to know my special love too." That's the message of the Book of Jonah, for example. Still, the Jews tended to regard the Messiah as their personal property.

The first believers, beginning with the apostles, were, of course, Jews. As they professed their faith in Jesus, however, they didn't immediately stop being Jewish. They kept right on worshiping in the synagogue and observing their Jewish traditions — along with following the Christian message and practices. They considered themselves Jews — who had found the Messiah, Jesus.

We might imagine them announcing, "Yes, I used to be Jewish but now I'm Christian." They wouldn't have dreamed of something like that. These Jewish Christians saw faith in Jesus as the *fulfillment* of their traditional Jewish faith. They saw no need to cancel their traditions or stop doing anything they had been doing as devout Jews.

This continued allegiance to Jewish traditions caused problems as Gentiles began accepting Jesus.

First of all, some Jewish Christians weren't entirely sure that Gentiles were supposed to be saved. After all, the Gentiles hadn't followed the true faith about God in previous centuries. Instead, they had accepted false gods and hadn't kept the great law of Moses, the Ten Commandments.

Before you think, "Wow, what a bunch of snobs those Jewish Christians were," examine some of your own attitudes. Pick out a couple countries that have policies and beliefs different from ours. Are you looking forward to sharing a heavenly racquetball court (or a celestial pizza or whatever) with folks from those places? Can you see yourself arriving in heaven on the same shuttle as one of those "foreigners," giving that person a big hug, and saying, "Isn't it great to be here together?"

Or would part of you get a secret little satisfaction out of the idea that maybe God'll waste 'em . . . or at least make them stay in one of heaven's economy motels (no movies, no pool) while you get the Ritz?

But if Gentiles were going to be accepted into the communities of Christian believers, then the Jewish Christians figured the Gentiles ought to get there the same way they did: by being Jewish first. That meant accepting Jewish dietary regulations (no pork, of course, among other things) and the practice of circumcision — the traditional, sacred sign of the Covenant.

Needless to say, Gentile men weren't crazy about getting circumcised (this was before hospitals, surgical knives, and anesthetics) and saw no purpose in it. So there was a great hassle over the central question, "Do you have to be Jewish (in customs and practices) in order to be Christian?"

Eventually it was solved, with the basic answer being "No." The Acts of the Apostles gives a fuller explanation of this discussion. This issue is also very important to keep in mind when reading many parts of Paul's Letters, particularly when he speaks about observance of the law. When Paul speaks about the law, he is not referring to the idea of right and wrong. Rather, he's speaking of the Jewish law, the entire code of traditionally Jewish practices that govern circumcision, dietary customs, and Sabbath regulations.

Learning about the many difficulties faced by the early Christians, it's amazing that Christianity worked at all. It had a lot going against it.

It must have had even more going *for* it.

What?

To find out, read the Gospels. They give us the amazing stories and teachings that form the foundation for our Christian beliefs and practices.

You say you've read them before. Great! Now read them again and again because the message never grows old. It is always new. Read them repeatedly and you will still learn new things on the hundredth reading.

12

It's About Time
We Started

Now that we've looked at people and life in the first century, it's time to look at the important Christian books written in that era. There are many ways that the books of the New Testament could be arranged. Someone concerned with dates and history might want the New Testament to begin with Mark's Gospel because it was written before the Gospel of Matthew. Others might suggest arranging Paul's Letters in chronological order rather than according to length. There are other arrangements that also make sense.

But it's no big thing. We're going to use the traditional ordering of the books in the New Testament. But you don't have to read the New Testament in that order. It would probably be better if you didn't.

Many study programs recommend beginning with the Gospel of Mark, the first and most direct of the Gospels, and then reading Acts. If you're using this book to help you with a class or course or study group, the teacher or leader has probably already given you an outline to follow.

You might keep these rules in mind as you form your own game plan for reading the New Testament.

Rule Number One: *Whatever New Testament "book" you're reading, read all of it, start to finish.* If possible (and it probably is), read it at least once straight through. It isn't that big a job in terms of reading. None of the New Testament documents is terribly long. Reading all of Mark, for example, is not like reading all of *Huckleberry Finn* or *War and Peace*. It takes slightly less than an hour.

When you're young, reading bits and pieces of the New Testament is probably all you can handle. But you're not an itty bitty munchkin anymore. Looking up just bits and pieces of the New Testament, especially the Gospels — a verse here, three or four verses there — can be like working as an usher at a busy theater. You see three minutes of a film during one showing, eight or nine during another, five during still another, and so on. Eventually you pick up the general idea of the film, but you never experience the impact of seeing it entirely, straight through. It's worth taking the time to read a document of the New Testament straight through in order to get that full and complete impact.

Rule Number Two: *Don't expect to understand everything right away* — and don't tune out the New Testament when you can't. This is not the sports or the comic page, for heaven's sake. You didn't understand everything about baseball the first time you picked up a bat or stuck a glove on your hand, either. You still had much to learn after the second or third or fortieth game, for that matter. Give it a chance. Give it lots of chances. (God has given *you* lots of chances.)

Rule Number Three: *Use a book* (like this one) *to help you understand the Scriptures, but don't read it instead of the New Testament*. For example, it's good to know the situation Paul encountered and addressed in his Letter to the Galatians. But nobody can skim over a few general ideas about Galatians, in this book or anywhere else, and claim that they truly understand what Paul said. To understand any of Paul's letters, you have to read that letter — over and over again.

The rest of this book will give you some background on each part of the New Testament and point out things to look for as you read it.

13

The Gospel According to Matthew

Author: Unknown
Date: A.D. 80–90

There's a second-century tradition (that's a story that made quite a few rounds) that the Apostle Matthew (the tax collector) wrote a Gospel in Aramaic. Maybe so — but if so, experts say it wasn't the one that we have in the Bible today, even though this one bears his name. Among other things, this Gospel seems to have undergone several revisions or redactions. It also borrows from many other sources, including Mark. That certainly wouldn't have been necessary if the actual Apostle Matthew, an eyewitness to Jesus' public life, had written this Gospel. But we'll call the author Matthew anyway.

Whoever he was, Matthew certainly knew the Jewish Scriptures exceptionally well and wrote for an audience of Jewish Christians who were also quite familiar with them. There are more Old Testament references in this Gospel than in any other, beginning with the ancestry or family record of Jesus.

This genealogy, which appears in chapter one, is an artificial device constructed from three groups of fourteen names taken from the historical books of the Old Testament. The list mentions many significant people but omits the names of some important kings. The numbers had a symbolic value that was clear to the original readers but that today's readers don't immediately grasp.

Matthew follows his genealogy with the Wise Men story. Now, if we get all hung up on whether or not three important foreigners actually pulled into Bethlehem on their camels, we're going to miss the whole point. What's important is that they are *Gentiles,* they come from *far away,* and they *acknowledge Jesus as king.* So, right after showing Jesus' Jewish origins, Matthew gives his audience the other side of the coin: Jesus is meant for all people throughout the world.

The central message in this Gospel is that Jesus is the Messiah-King foretold in the Jewish Scriptures who will bring salvation to all people. Matthew does everything he can to affirm Jesus as "the real thing" for his Jewish Christian audience, especially by presenting Jesus as the son of David. He's also careful to note that Joseph is not the physical father of Jesus.

The Gospel also presents Jesus as the new Moses. Just as Moses led a captive people out of slavery into the Promised Land, Jesus has done the same thing. He has led all people out of slavery to sin and into the promised land of salvation.

The Gospel also presents Jesus as a great teacher, someone very much like Moses whom the Jews saw as their great teacher. In Matthew's Gospel there are several sections where Jesus gives long, instructive speeches, often called "discourses." Matthew's Gospel is structured around these discourses. The longest is the "Sermon on the Mount" in chapters 5–7. It's the largest (and best-known) single collection of the teachings of Jesus. Matthew seems to have compiled it from several sources. Among many other things, it contains the Beatitudes and the "golden rule."

In parts of the great discourse, the words of Jesus reverse what people have learned in the past. Several times Jesus says, "You have heard . . . but I say to you that. . . . " This fits in with Matthew's theme of Jesus fulfilling the Old Testament tradition and then issuing a challenge to Christians to go beyond "the basics" to the "law of love."

A series of miracle stories follows the sermon; the purpose of placing them next might have been to affirm the authority of Jesus' teaching. These aren't just isolated stories to show that Jesus had supernatural power, though. Each story confirms the basic meaning of Jesus' mission by demonstrating that Jesus is the fulfillment of prophecy and a person to be believed.

There are also many parables in Matthew; chapter 13 is particularly famous for the "kingdom" parables.

Jesus didn't invent parables. They were an old Jewish tradition, a simple means to impart wisdom to ordinary people. A parable could be anything from a short proverb to a relatively long story with symbolic characters and places. The parables of Jesus are usually short stories, although some are simply a few brief verses of comparison.

The parables allow for comparison between ourselves and the characters in the story, between our lives and theirs. They are intended to make us think about how we're living and how we might change, correct, and improve our lives.

The "kingdom of heaven" is another important theme in Matthew's Gospel. (The other Gospels call it the "Kingdom of God." But Matthew is writing for believers who still keep the Jewish tradition of not actually saying the name of God out loud. The two phrases mean the same thing.) The parables of the kingdom all share a common theme: A mysterious but real force has entered the world. Some people become a part of it; others oppose, reject, or lose it — to their later regret.

There are many more things that could be said about the Gospel of Matthew. Entire books are written about this one Gospel. These ideas about the focus, style, and context of this Gospel are enough to get you started. Now read the Gospel of Matthew!

14

The Gospel According to Mark

Author: A companion of Paul, probably the "John-Mark" mentioned in Acts
Date: A.D. 60–75

In many ways the Gospel of Mark is quite similar to the Gospel of Matthew. Nearly every story in Mark is retold in Matthew. At the same time, there are some very clear differences in emphasis, outlook, and purpose between the two Gospels.

Mark doesn't share Matthew's concern about Jesus as the new Moses. Mark also doesn't use long discourses in the same way as Matthew. Rather, Mark is very concerned to address the questions of who Jesus was and is. His whole Gospel is arranged with this in mind.

In some TV detective shows, *you* see the crime being committed right at the beginning. You know "who done it." But none of the characters in the show have this knowledge. As you watch the show, you see them gradually figuring out what you knew at the beginning.

Mark's Gospel is a bit like this. In chapter one, verse one, Mark tells us that Jesus is the son of God. Then the first part of his Gospel is filled with stories of things Jesus did, particularly many miracle stories. When someone goes around expelling demons and curing diseases, the obvious question is, "Who is he?" After many of these episodes, people, including the apostles, ask, "Who *is* this?" (We, of course, know.)

The questions keep coming until Jesus himself asks the question of Peter, who says, "You are the Messiah!" (Mark 8:27-30).

Jesus lets the apostles know that this is correct — but also that they haven't the slightest idea of what the mission of the Messiah is all about. He instructs them (and therefore us) gradually.

The answer to the question of Jesus' identity is repeated at his death on the Cross. This time, though, it's a Roman centurion who says that Jesus is the son of God (see Mark 15:39). The centurion's response highlights the fact that Mark was writing for Gentile Christians, possibly in Rome itself.

Since his audience is only vaguely familiar with Jewish customs and background, Mark has Jesus explain many points that Matthew could presume his Jewish readers would understand. Jesus' explanation of how the Messiah will have to suffer (the apostles aren't too happy with this news) links the idea of living the Christian life with the reality of human suffering. This brings consolation to Mark's Gentile Christian audience who suffer many persecutions because of their faith.

The idea of a suffering servant who brings life through death, a key theme in Mark, has a strong Old Testament background. Chapter 53 of Isaiah is one of the clearest examples. In Jesus' time, though, people had pretty well discarded the idea of a suffering, dying Messiah. Mark's Gospel, in its simple, direct, and very graphic way, recalls the link between Jesus and the suffering servant of Isaiah.

Mark's account of the Resurrection events is extremely brief. Most experts believe his original manuscript ended at 16:8 and that the following verses (Mark 16:9-20) are the work of a later editor. If that is true, the original Gospel of Mark contains no Resurrection appearances and no descriptions of astonished joy among Jesus' followers. But maybe Mark intends it that way, figuring they are unnecessary.

After all, we already know in chapter one, verse one that Jesus is the Son of God.

15

The Gospel According to Luke

Author: Luke
Date: A.D. 70–90

Luke is probably the only Gentile author who writes in the New Testament. He was apparently a Greek, a close friend of Paul's, and very likely the "doctor" Paul mentions in his Letter to the Colossians.

It's really important to remember that Luke's Gospel is Volume I of a two-volume series; the second is the Acts of the Apostles. Many Scripture programs recommend that these two books be read together (and, yes, straight through if possible). That's a good suggestion.

Luke wrote for Gentile Christians. Yet, the first two chapters of his Gospel are full of incidents with Jewish references and backgrounds. It is Luke who tells us of the Annunciation and Visitation, gives us the fullest Nativity account, and presents three major events before the beginning of Jesus' public life.

Luke is telling his audience, "This is terrific, folks: We're part of an incredible movement in history — God reaching down into the days of our lives and working out a terrific plan of salvation through these special people." While there can be some question about the historical accuracy of his description of the events in these two chapters, there is no mistaking the underlying message of salvation.

The *Spirit* plays a very large role in all of Luke's writings. God working through the Spirit is a constant theme in both his Gospel and in Acts. John the Baptizer is filled with the Spirit; the Spirit overshadows Mary; Elizabeth and Zechariah are likewise filled with the Spirit; the Spirit leads Jesus into the desert, makes him heal people, and fills him with wisdom.

Luke also emphasizes God reaching into history through his Spirit to form a community, a group, a church. It seems as though some of Luke's audience may have lost their sense of "who we are" (just as some Christians have today). Luke makes it clear to them (and to us) that salvation comes through membership in this Spirit-filled community.

The Gospel of Luke contains a greater atmosphere of *joy* over the events of salvation than is present in the Gospels of Matthew or Mark. (The canticles of Mary and Zechariah in Luke, chapter one, are good examples of this spirit of joy.) This, too, is consistent with Luke's purpose of trying to restore a feeling of optimism to his audience. After all, they lived in a world where the culture was Greek and the politics were Roman. It couldn't have been easy.

Still another characteristic of Luke's Gospel is something called "universalism." In plain English, this means "Everybody's invited" — salvation is open to all people. Several incidents and parables which only Luke reports demonstrate this. An example is the Good Samaritan, where a less-than-pure Jew lives out the love of neighbor demanded of Jesus' followers (Luke 10:25-37).

The idea of universal salvation is not just a national or ethnic theme. Luke places great emphasis on Jesus as the friend of sinners. He shows that Jesus has come not to gather a small group of holy people, but to bring salvation to everyone, regardless of their current state of spiritual health.

Luke alone gives us the parable of a vineyard owner who has patience with a fig tree that isn't producing fruit (Luke 13:6-9). In Luke, Jesus places a sinful, but repentant, woman above his very proper host and fellow guests (Luke 7:36-50). He deliberately seeks the friendship of Zacchaeus, a particularly despised tax collector (Luke 19:1-10). He promises salvation to one of the criminals crucified with him (Luke 23:39-43).

Chapter 15 is devoted entirely to this theme. The one lost sheep is so important that the good shepherd leaves the ninety-nine that haven't messed up in order to find it. A woman rejoices more over finding her one lost silver piece than over the nine she didn't lose. Crowning it all is the parable of the prodigal son and the forgiving father.

Luke gives us several appearances of Jesus after his Resurrection. Each one leads to the realization expressed in chapter 24, verse 34: It's *true* . . . the Lord *has* risen!

16

The Gospel According to John

Author: Probably a group of the disciples of the apostle John
Date: A.D. 90–110

There is quite a bit of speculation among serious New Testament scholars on exactly how many different people are referred to as "John" in the New Testament. Is John, the brother of James, the same as the Beloved Disciple, and are either of them the "John" who is believed to be the author of the fourth Gospel? One of these people named John *may* have written or orally composed an early version of this Gospel. There's a good bit of evidence, however, that the present version was revised by other people, probably his community of followers.

Chapter 21 is a good example of this later editing. It seems to be an afterthought. The style is considerably different. Instead of speaking very solemnly as he does throughout most of the Gospel, Jesus talks in a folksy manner.

A similar situation can be noted in the two conclusions to the long discourse Jesus gives at the Last Supper. In John 14:31, Jesus seems to end his instruction and announce that they're going to leave the room where they've eaten. He continues the instruction in the very next verse, however, and the actual leaving happens in 18:1.

Since this was the last of the four Gospels to be written, you might expect it to show deeper insights into the meaning of the life and mission of Jesus. When you read the Gospel with this in mind, you won't be disappointed. Be prepared for a real change from Mark, Matthew, and Luke.

Imagine it this way: Four sons produce written tributes to their father. Three of them concentrate more on events of the father's life. One may emphasize events which show the father as a decisive man of action. Another may point out how the father's actions are similar to those of important ancestors. Still another may emphasize events which show him as loving and affectionate. The fourth son uses a different style and produces a lyrical poem. It's based on the events of the father's life, of course, but it spends far more time interpreting their meaning. While this is not a perfect parallel to the four Gospels, it may help you understand the differences between the Synoptic Gospels and the Gospel according to John.

From the very beginning of this Gospel, often referred to as the "prologue," you can tell we're dealing not only with poetic writing but with actual theology — deep reflection on the meaning of Jesus.

This prologue talks about Jesus as the *Word* of God. This has a vastly different significance among the Jews than it does for us (until we understand the concept). A word to them is thought of as an actual living thing, having a life of its own after it has been brought into existence by being spoken. (Isaiah 55:11 gives a good example.)

The actual word used to express "word" is the Greek *logos*. To a certain group of Greek philosophers, the *logos* held the whole universe together and gave it meaning and purpose.

Notice how heavy the territory is getting . . . and we're only into the first few verses.

But don't let that scare you away from John's Gospel. His words are poetic and simple and rich and deep all at the same time. If there's something you don't completely understand, you're in company with some of the world's best scholars who are still studying this Gospel.

The Gospel is often divided into two main parts. In the first, chapters 1–12, John talks about the signs Jesus gave that indicate who he is. Signs here include really almost everything he did — his miracles, obviously, but also his teachings, and his life in general.

Chapters 5, 6, 9, and 10 illustrate this pattern in John's Gospel: A miracle story is followed by a fairly long discourse or teaching. In these lessons, the significance of Jesus — who he is and what he does as Messiah — and his relationship to the Father are common themes.

The second part, chapters 13–21, is sometimes called "The Hour of Jesus" or "The Book of Glory." Imagine a movie in which the first part shows the hero as a very special person — especially gifted, especially good. Then he or she meets rising opposition. Finally, the setting, the music, the very plot of the story itself, and everything you see and hear on the screen practically announces that *the time is here . . . the moment has come* for the showdown. The hero will confront the opposition in a dramatic climax . . . and you know that even if the hero has to sacrifice his life for the cause, the side of good will win. The outcome may be tragic in some ways, but it will be glorious overall.

Now I know that sounds like Hollywood, but it may give you a clear picture of what happens in the second part of this Gospel. The theme of glory is especially central to chapter 17 when Jesus speaks of the special glory which he and his Father will experience and then share with all people.

It's good for us to remember this time of glory because what's about to happen is not going to look very glorious at all by human standards. We see a beaten, bloody, dying man nailed to a cross. But Jesus does rise, and the Gospel records several appearances.

You can read John's Gospel many times and still be captivated by the poetic sweep, each time finding something that didn't strike you before.

17

The Acts
of the Apostles

Author: Luke
Date: A.D. 80–90

The title can be a bit misleading. This New Testament book really doesn't tell us much about the original apostles. A brief mention in the first chapter is the last we hear about most of them.

The other part is extremely on target. There's definitely a lot of action in Acts — riots, jailbreaks, courtroom drama, midnight escapes, shipwreck.

Luke didn't write this book simply to tell an interesting story, however. He's trying to show that something special is happening in the world. He wants everyone to know that the Church, the new community united by faith in the risen Jesus, is spreading throughout the world through the action of the Spirit.

Luke selects only those events which best illustrate his themes. The theme of *universalism* that figured prominently in Luke's Gospel is even more important in Acts. In a way, it's *the* theme of Acts. Luke sees a clear progression in the spread of the faith. What begins as a small, exclusively Jewish Christian community in Jerusalem, spreads to Samaria (Samaritans aren't pure Jews, remember), up to Antioch where some Gentiles join, and then finally to many Gentile communities around the Mediterranean.

Luke begins his story with the Ascension and then situates the apostles (with Mary) in Jerusalem. We can imagine them huddled together, joyful that Jesus is risen but confused about what to do from this point on. It's as though they've just inherited a huge fortune but they're not sure what to do with it.

Then it happens. One event changes this small, prayerful, but not very public, group into dynamic preachers: The Spirit comes upon them as Jesus had promised. It's a dramatic scene. A small group of loyal but confused believers become bold, decisive missionaries filled with enthusiasm. They begin to gain converts from many different backgrounds. They get people to believe in something that, on the surface, doesn't make much sense: A suffering, crucified Savior died and came back to life.

The community grows as people hear and accept the basic message, called the "kerygma," of Jesus. You'll find six examples of the kerygma in Acts: 2:14-36, 3:12-26, 4:8-12, 5:29-32, 10:34-43, and 13:16-41. In the first five, Peter is speaking; the last one belongs to Paul.

Notice something about each of these kerygmatic speeches. Nowhere does Peter or anyone else attempt to prove what he's saying. There's no attempt to give lots of persuasive details about the appearances of Jesus after the Resurrection, for example. This is called "prophetic announcement." The apostles invite people to *believe* the religious truth they're offering, not run it through a computer and see if it comes out making perfect sense.

Luke points out how Peter and John catch a lot of heat from their preaching. At first they're let off with just a warning, but later they end up in jail, escape miraculously, and keep right on preaching. Of course, these episodes mirror the opposition Jesus himself experienced.

Because of their preaching, Peter and John were called to appear before the Sanhedrin, the highest council of Jewish authority. This ruling body was composed of elders from the important Jewish families, high priests, former high priests, and Scribes, who were mostly Pharisees. The Roman government allowed the Jewish Sanhedrin to enforce local and religious laws as long as it did not interfere with Roman authority. Exactly how powerful it was we're not sure.

Chapters 6 and 7 of Acts belong to Stephen, the first deacon. He's arrested for preaching and teaching about Jesus and finds himself in court before the Sanhedrin, suffering the same fate as Peter and John. Luke records a long speech and attributes it to Stephen. While we can't be absolutely certain that Stephen actually delivered this speech on this occasion, it is clear that these words represent Stephen's thinking. In this speech, which certainly did not help Stephen's popularity rating with the Sanhedrin, he summarizes Jewish history and gives it a definite slant. He shows how God's people have done a pretty miserable job of heeding God's message in the past, and how recently they've fouled up royally by rejecting Jesus, the Messiah.

For his honesty and his faith, Stephen is stoned to death.

In chapter 8, Luke begins to record the expansion of the Gospel beyond Jerusalem — first to Samaritans and then to an Ethiopian. While this man is not Jewish, he's not totally a Gentile either. He represents people the Jews called ''God-fearers'': They believed in the one true God and used the Jewish Scriptures, but didn't get circumcised or follow other Jewish laws.

Chapter 9 presents that dramatic, world-changing reversal: Paul meets the risen Jesus and is converted to the very faith he's trying so hard to destroy. This incident is also mentioned in Acts, chapters 22 and 26, and in 1 Corinthians 15:8-9.

There's little difference in detail among the three accounts. The words of Jesus are nearly identical. Luke seems to treat this as a genuine historical event rather than as a means of relating an intense religious experience or soul-searching on the part of Paul.

In all three episodes of Paul's conversion, Jesus identifies himself with his Church and his followers. Perhaps this initial encounter with Jesus is the source of Paul's explanation, in Ephesians and Colossians, of the Church as the Body of Christ.

Paul's first experiences carrying the Christian banner meet with disaster. But there's this advantage at least: With Paul no longer spearheading a Christian persecution, the Church experiences a brief period of peace.

Full acceptance of Gentiles into the Christian community begins with a Roman centurion named Cornelius. His baptism, which may symbolize many Gentile conversions, causes some distress for the Christians in Jerusalem.

Acts 12:19-26 is such a low-key passage we could read right past it without realizing its significance. The Church is established at Antioch in Syria (north of Jerusalem), where Jewish converts are joined by many Gentiles. In time, Antioch would become a pillar of the Christian world equal to Jerusalem.

Paul and Barnabas set out from Antioch on their first great missionary journey (Read Acts 13:1—14:27). They develop a radical policy: When a Jewish audience rejects what they say, they deliberately turn to the Gentiles. To their wonderment, they very often meet with greater success than they had with their own Jewish people.

Nearly every edition of the Bible contains maps of Paul's journeys. If all these journeys are illustrated on the same map, with different markings for each, they may be difficult to follow. But it's worth the effort. You'll find that sometimes Paul retraces his steps (look for arrows in both directions on the same line).

After the return from the first journey, Luke relates the "Council of Jerusalem" story. The issue at stake (both in Antioch and Jerusalem) was whether or not Gentiles had to adopt at least the basic Jewish traditions such as circumcision in order to enter the Christian community. (We've covered the background to this in Chapter 11, "Those First Christian Folks.")

After serious discussion and even open disagreement between the apostles, it is decided that Gentile Christians need not adopt Jewish practices. This is indeed a major breakthrough credited to the work of the Holy Spirit.

Paul's second journey is recounted in Acts 15:36—18:22. He

and Barnabas have argued over John-Mark, and they separate. (They'll become friends again later.) Silas is Paul's companion on this journey.

In Acts 16:10-17, you'll find the first of the "we sections" of Acts as the story switches to a "first person" narrator. This will happen again in Acts 20:5-15, 21:1-18, and 27:1-28. The likeliest explanation is that Luke really did accompany Paul for some part of his second and third journeys.

In Lystra, where things had gone disastrously before, Paul meets Timothy, who becomes a key figure in the Church of that region. In Philippi, Paul and Silas get a scourging so suddenly and violently that they don't even have time to appeal to their Roman citizenship, which would have prevented it. The local Roman officials are upset when they find out what they have done in haste to these Roman citizens. There's another great escape from prison episode in chapter 16.

After very little success in Thessalonica and Athens, Paul moves to Corinth and settles there for almost two years. This becomes the most famous of the Christian communities founded directly by Paul. It is here that Paul officially and publicly announces that he's offering his message exclusively to the Gentiles (Acts 18:6).

While Paul's third missionary journey covers much territory, Acts concentrates primarily on his work in Ephesus. There are exciting scenes here, too, particularly the riot of the silversmiths, who see Paul as a serious threat to their economy (Acts 19:23-40). The goddess mentioned here is an Asian version of the Greek goddess, Artemis, whom the Romans called Diana. The temple dedicated to her, the Artemision, was one of the seven wonders of the ancient world.

Paul feels an urging to return to Jerusalem even though he suspects he'll run into trouble there, and that's precisely the case. In fact, what happens to Paul as a result of incidents in Jerusalem fills the rest of the pages of Acts. From this point on, the story is easy to follow.

The vow which Paul has taken is known as the Nazirite vow. (Acts 21:15-40 and Numbers 6:1-21 explain this incident and the nature of the vow.) What's interesting is that Paul, in spite of being the Apostle to the Gentiles, has undertaken a completely voluntary Jewish practice.

When Paul is about to be interrogated and whipped, he rather casually mentions his Roman citizenship (Acts 22:22-29). Notice the Roman commander responding instantly and worrying because Paul has even been tied up. It is the commander's job to ensure any Roman citizen's safety and right to a full legal hearing. That's why Paul is transferred to Caesarea (Acts 23:12-35).

Felix, the procurator in that locale, has a reputation for cruelty and incompetence. Complaints even reach Rome about him, and some historians think his harsh policies brought about the Jewish rebellion of A.D. 66-70. Eventually he is recalled to Rome, but found not guilty.

Festus replaces Felix and refers Paul's case to the Jewish puppet king, Agrippa. Using his right as a Roman citizen, Paul demands that his case be personally tried at the imperial court in Rome. The journey to Rome (it's not peaceful!) shows Luke at his storytelling best. This section is just plain fun to read.

In Rome, Paul is held under house arrest and is allowed to preach to anyone who comes to him. Luke ends his story simply by saying that Paul stayed there two years. We really don't know for sure what happened to him after that.

Some people find that disappointing, considering that Luke has just given us an exceptionally dramatic series of events leading up to Paul's coming to Rome for trial. Others find it very appropriate that Acts ends "open-ended": The story of faith has not ended. The Gospel endures and the Good News spreads day by day.

18

Letters from Paul and His Closest Friends

Huge variety here, folks.

Some of the New Testament Letters are similar to the letters you write, complete with apologies ("Sorry I haven't written," "Sorry we haven't been able to get together,") and greetings ("Say hello to . . . " "Give my best to . . . "). Others are very formal and sound more like a textbook than a letter. Some can be read in less than five minutes; others are much longer.

Enjoy!

Romans

Author: Paul
Date: About A.D. 58

The Letter to the Romans is not really typical of Paul's Letters. Most of them were written to people he knew and loved. He wrote this Letter while in Corinth before he went to visit Rome. The style is a little stiff, just as yours probably would be if you wrote to people you've never actually met.

In Romans, Paul tackles the thorny problem you're familiar with by now: the relationship between the Jewish faith and faith in Jesus. He links that theme to an even bigger theme: the issue of evil and sin.

Paul tries to show that *everybody* is under the influence of sin, both Jews and Gentiles. Release from the power of sin comes when people have faith in Jesus.

In the process of explaining this, Paul uses some theologically "high tech" words like justification and salvation.

In a nutshell, Paul explains that God is completely holy; people are not. Something has to happen to bring or restore people to a state where they can be accepted into God's presence. "Justification" is that something. It happens when Jesus dies, rises, and offers us the chance to have faith in him. Now it's possible for us to make it to heaven if we believe in him. Without Jesus, it isn't possible.

"Salvation" is what happens to us when we act on our faith in Jesus and live as Christians each day. But we can only live as Christians if we first have faith in the risen Lord who died for us. Making it, in other words, is a gift or a grace from God. It's not a matter of chalking up clever credit points in God's grade book and feeling pretty cool about being promoted to heaven on our own merit.

In this discussion, Paul explains that salvation comes through belief in the grace of God and the actions of Jesus Christ, and *not* simply through observance of the Jewish law. Paul notes that he is not anti-law and points out that the "father" of Judaism itself, Abraham, began by *believing. Then* he was circumcised (followed the law). In case anyone thinks that the way a person acts no longer matters ("Wow, this getting to heaven is a piece of cake — all you do is say 'I believe!' "), Paul quickly explains his meaning in chapter 6 and again in chapters 12–15.

First Corinthians

Author: Paul
Date: About A.D. 55

Beginning a Christian community in Corinth was a little like beginning one at Times Square in the heart of New York City. Corinth may have been the Roman Empire's number one Sin City. Paul's success there was very unlikely by human standards, but it happened.

Paul wrote this Letter after having been gone from Corinth for several years and learning that all sorts of problems had developed. Some of them were doctrinal (what to believe) and some were moral (how to behave). Considering that they were living in the middle of exceptionally wild times, we can understand how the Corinthians had difficulty staying straight. Paul spoke forcefully and yet with love as he told them that they were behaving like pagans and in need of personal reform.

On top of the moral problems, there were bitter divisions among the Corinthian Christians. Different groups claimed allegiance to different leaders and apparently acted as though their group contained the *real* Christians.

This Letter is one of Paul's greatest literary achievements. He points out that truth is contained in the irony of a crucified Savior — and any attempt to soften or sweeten this idea is stupid. He constantly refers to real and false wisdom, strength, and respectability.

Paul's favorite way of thinking about the Church is to see it as the body of Christ. He develops and extends this comparison in First Corinthians. For many people, the high point of the Letter is Paul's description of love in chapter 13.

In addressing another issue, Paul notes that many Greeks, including some of the Corinthians, have some doubts about the resurrection of the body. This leads them to an attitude of "party hearty because when you're gone, you're gone." Paul re-explains the belief in the resurrection of the body. Apparently the most common question, then, is the same as now: "How? What's it going to be like?" Paul's answer in chapter 15 says, "Don't worry about it. God can handle it."

Second Corinthians

Author: Paul
Date: About A.D. 57

Paul is concerned that he hasn't been able to pay a second visit to the Corinthians and that this will lessen his credibility as an apostle. Much of the first seven chapters are devoted to a defense of his position and his actions. Paul's authority apparently is being rejected by someone in the Corinthian community.

After reading Paul's compliments to his audience in chapters 8 and 9, we're positively jolted by chapter 10. Is this the same Paul? He makes accusations and becomes positively sarcastic. Chapters 10 through 13 of Second Corinthians are so different in tone from chapters 1 through 9 that some scholars think this may have been part of another letter, written before the first part of this one.

In chapters 10 through 13, Paul writes about those who have come to Corinth preaching a different gospel and considering themselves superior to him. Paul uses a sarcastic term for them, which the *New American Bible* translates beautifully as "the super apostles." At times, Paul goes beyond being defensive to being almost outraged. Yet, throughout this passage Paul is not trying to pin missionary medals on himself. He's only concerned that his beloved Corinthians stick with the truth and do not become disillusioned.

Galatians

Author: Paul
Date: As early as A.D. 48
or as late as A.D. 55

If you read the New Testament books in order, you'll probably say "Here we go again" when you come to Galatians. The problems Paul faces are getting pretty familiar. (But don't skip past Galatians for that reason.) As he was forced to do in the Second Letter to the Corinthians, Paul defends himself as a messenger of the Gospel (chapters 1 and 2).

As he did in Romans, he compares and contrasts the relationship between the Jewish law and the Christian faith. Some people in the Galatian community have begun to think that following the Jewish law code is the way to salvation. Paul uses extremely strong language in opposing this position (chapter 3).

This leads Paul to talk about the true meaning of Christian freedom. He compares being a Christian to becoming an adult son or daughter of God, as opposed to being like small children who still have to keep a lot of little regulations "for their own good" (chapter 4).

As he has before, Paul is quick to point out that the freedom he's talking about is definitely not the "anything goes" type of freedom. In case anybody doesn't know the things that a free-from-the-law Christian must avoid, Paul lists them pretty bluntly (chapters 5 and 6).

Ephesians

Author: Uncertain
Date: About A.D. 62

There are no personal greetings in this Letter, and the tone is pretty stiff and formal. That's why it's doubtful that Paul is the author. It's not likely he would have written such a formal letter to people he knew and had lived with for quite a while.

At the time of this Letter, a lot of "mystery religions" were going around the Roman Empire. Today we'd call them unusual cults or something like that. One of the most popular was a thing called "Gnosticism," which had many varieties. Gnostics believed that salvation came through secret knowledge. Some of them considered material things to be evil: Only the spirit was good.

Some people were getting these things mixed up with the Christian faith. Among other things, the Letter to the Ephesians tries to set the audience straight. If you like to see your Christian faith set in a background of cosmic stuff, read Ephesians.

Toward the end of Ephesians, there are two passages that sometimes get the whole New Testament in trouble. They talk about wives being submissive to their husbands and slaves obeying their masters (Ephesians 5:22-33; 6:5-9).

You'll need the help of a more detailed book to understand fully how those passages are interpreted for today's world. Keep in mind the fact that this letter was not written originally for twentieth-century American Christians. It was written for first-century Ephesian Christians. Some of the items in the Letter need to be understood in that context. What applies to our twentieth-century situation, however, are the *ideas* or principles beneath the surface.

This simple example might help. In the 1930s, an aunt might have written to her niece, "I do hope you have a good time when that nice young man takes you to dinner. Remember, you must wear your gloves."

Wearing dress gloves (not the keep-warm type) on a formal occasion was proper for women at that time. It was the "right" thing to do. Today things have changed. Gloves are not worn in that situation. That part of the advice (the surface behavior) would no longer be practical. There's an idea beneath the surface, however, that gives a timeless suggestion: Honor your date and yourself by dressing properly for the occasion.

Philippians

Author: Paul
Date: Disputed; as early as A.D. 53 or as late as A.D. 62

Paul wrote this Letter from prison, but scholars are not sure exactly where and when he was in prison. He may have been in prison more than once. Since he was certainly in prison when he wrote this, it is called one of the "Captivity Letters." (Colossians, Ephesians, and Philemon are the other Letters written from prison.)

Paul does not offer innovative or extensive teaching in the Letter to the Philippians. It tends to be more of a personal, folksy letter. But six verses of it are extremely famous: 2:6-11. This is probably an early Christian hymn of praise which Paul quotes in his Letter. It is much more than a simple little ditty of a hymn. It provides theologians with clear ideas about who Jesus is, how he is related to the Father, and how he is both human and divine.

Colossians

Author: Perhaps Paul
Date: Between A.D. 58 and 63

Definite differences in vocabulary leave some scholars wondering if Paul wrote this Letter himself. Regardless of that, we have a Letter similar in focus to the Letter to the Ephesians.

This Letter uses the word "mystery" to refer to God's plan for salvation. Like the Ephesians, the Colossians are touched by Gnostic influences. We can see it in references such as Colossians 2:8 and 2:15. It suggests that some Colossians had put their faith in creatures that had power over humans but that were not as powerful as God. To counteract these beliefs, the author repeats the teaching that Jesus and only Jesus is the Savior who has reconciled people with God. Jesus is presented not only as a Savior but also as a divine cosmic principle. Through him the universe was created and through him salvation has been won.

First Thessalonians

Author: Paul
Date: A.D. 50 or 51

This is the earliest piece of writing in the New Testament. Paul is writing to the community he had to leave hastily at night because of intense opposition, and he freely expresses his worries about them.

The big issue in First Thessalonians concerns the second coming of Christ. A lot of people in this community are rather certain that the end of the world is going to occur very soon. They're worried about their relatives who have died and who will not witness the final coming. They're wondering if that's going to make a difference.

Basically, Paul tells them not to worry. God will take care of everything. Just hang in there, live straight, and everything will be OK both for them and their deceased relatives.

Great advice, good answer. It might be the case that perhaps Paul himself, at this early point in his development, thought the second coming might be pretty soon.

Second Thessalonians

Author: Paul
Date: About A.D. 52

Paul continues his consideration of the same problem in this brief Letter. Some Thessalonians still think that the great heavenly roundup is coming very soon — so soon that they apparently decide it isn't worth holding down a job since this world is about to end. Paul again tells them to stop being concerned about this and get back to making progress in the Christian life — and back to work.

First Timothy

Author: Uncertain
Date: Uncertain but rather late; close to A.D. 100

The two Letters to Timothy and the one to Titus are called the "Pastoral Letters." They talk more about the organization and government of the community than about beliefs and morals. Much of this First Letter to Timothy is filled with practical advice about dealing with individuals and particular groups of people in the Christian community.

The conduct and treatment of widows was a big issue in the Church at Ephesus at the time of this Letter. Because women didn't have careers with which to support themselves, they were often dependent on the community for their welfare. Sometimes the community neglected their needs, but other times the widows apparently took advantage of the community's support.

The Letter is especially interesting because it shows that in some Christian communities a governmental structure had been established that included a bishop, presbyters (priests), and deacons. While some communities might have been less structured, the community at Ephesus, led by Timothy, had a rather definite organizational structure.

Second Timothy

Author: Same as First Timothy
Date: Same as First Timothy

The ideas here are very similar to those in the First Letter to Timothy: Hang in there and stick with the truth, even if it doesn't make you popular.

Titus

Author: Same as First Timothy
Date: Same as First Timothy

This repeats many of the ideas contained in First Timothy, only in briefer fashion. It provides another glimpse at the organization of an early Christian community.

Philemon

Author: Paul
Date: A.D. 56–62

This may be a completely private letter or a letter written to a very small group of people. It's amazing that it was preserved at all. Paul writes to Philemon (and two other people named Apphia and Archippus) about Onesimus, Philemon's slave who ran away. Paul has met Onesimus, converted him to the faith, and now is sending him back to his master. But neither Paul nor Onesimus want Philemon to deal out the harsh treatment legally permitted for a runaway slave.

Paul either thought that returning the slave was the right thing to do, or that not returning the slave merely invited eventual disaster. As in other passages, he doesn't call slavery wrong. But he does call Onesimus a *brother* to Philemon. For the times, that was a radical statement that might have caused Christians to rethink in some small way their attitudes toward the practice of slavery.

19

And More Letters

Besides the Letters written by Paul and his close friends and associates, there are eight other New Testament Letters written in the first one hundred or so years after Jesus' death. Like Paul's Letters, they reflect many concerns and teachings of the apostles and the early Church.

Hebrews

Author: Uncertain
Date: About A.D. 70

Like Romans, this is heavy stuff, only more so. It's abstract and full of theology. In a way, the first four verses introduce the main theme and, in a sense, summarize the rest of the Letter. (But don't try reading them and expect to understand Hebrews.)

The audience is obviously a group of Jewish Christians. They may have been having trouble understanding the relationship between the animal sacrifices which were a big part of their Jewish faith (and the role of the priest who offered them) and the sacrifice of Jesus on the Cross.

To make sense out of the Letter to the Hebrews, you need to understand something about sacrifice, which is a really complex subject. Some type of sacrifice is found in almost every religion. The worshiper brings something of value, nearly always something living — an animal — to a special place, usually an altar. Here the offering is killed — sacrificed — and often the blood is used for some special ceremonial action.

This act does several things. First, it shows the person's willingness to give everything, even life itself, back to God, who is symbolized by the altar. Second, it strengthens the bond between the person and God. Third, it often includes the idea of making up for sins.

Frequently, the gift which has been given up to God is then given back to the person who made the sacrifice. In the all-important annual Passover Sacrifice, the animal which is sacrificed is then shared in a special meal.

The Letter to the Hebrews shows that the sacrifices of the Old Law are intended to pave the way for the final sacrifice offered by Jesus, who is both priest (official offerer of the sacrifice) and victim (the sacrifice itself). The sacrifice of Jesus is the perfect sacrifice while the Old Testament sacrifices are imperfect. Jesus' sacrifice brings salvation and forgiveness to all people in all times and all places while the sacrifices of the Old Law have merit only for those directly involved in the act of sacrifice.

James

Author: Uncertain; perhaps the James who was the leader of the Christians in Jerusalem
Date: Also uncertain; between A.D. 60 and 80

Does Jesus carry people to heaven automatically as long as they *really* believe in him? Or do people have to *do* something besides believe?

It might be the case that those questions try to separate two sides of a coin, which can't be separated. In other words, is it possible to believe — really believe — but still not do good things as a result of believing? Or is it possible to do good things for people without being a person of faith?

Good questions. Think about them both before and after you read James. There's not much doubt about what James thinks, though.

First Peter

Author: Uncertain; perhaps a close disciple of Peter
Date: As early as A.D. 65, or as late as A.D. 95

This is a Letter full of advice on how to behave as a Christian in a world that thinks Christians are weird. Some people think the Letter may have been intended as practical advice for newly baptized Christians. The readers of this Letter didn't have it easy, whether from actual persecution or simply from general disbelief and hassling. A lot of attention is given to the mystery of suffering.

If you ever got put down, kicked out of the "cool" group, or took some kind of heat precisely because you did what was *right*, First Peter is a great Letter to read.

Second Peter

Author: Uncertain
Date: Uncertain; probably rather late, around A.D. 100

This Letter concentrates on two main ideas. First, the Letter explains the meaning of the second coming of Christ. It says that this is a very real event, but it doesn't say that it is coming soon. Second, the Letter urges Christians to resist false but attractive ideas. Apparently quite a few people, after accepting and living a Christian lifestyle, were returning to a "life is party time" and "if it feels good, do it" lifestyle. The last verse of chapter 2 borrows a somewhat gross but effective sentence from the Book of Proverbs to describe such people.

First John

Author: See the Gospel according to John
Date: A.D. 90–100

The Letters of John have the same references to light and darkness that we find in John's Gospel. In the Letters, however, these images are linked with the idea of love for others. The author is writing to a community which is having its problems, both with understanding the truths of the faith and with sticking together and behaving decently toward one another.

The theme of love is central to the beautifully written, often quoted section of this Letter (1 John 4:7-21). The author is particularly blunt about the need to love others as an absolutely necessary sign of one's genuine love of God. If we do not love our neighbors, we are liars to claim that we love God.

This Letter is the main source, incidentally, for the term "anti-Christ." Some folks make a big deal out of guessing who is or might be the anti-Christ. They identify it with Hitler or Communism or an undefined monster still lurking in our future. But the Letter is certainly not a prediction for the twentieth century, and it's not likely that the author is talking about one, specific, personal anti-Christ. The author is being generic here, as we can tell from 4:18 and 4:22. Quite likely, the anti-Christ was — and is — anyone who teaches things opposed to what Jesus taught.

Second John

Author: A man who calls himself "the Elder";
probably a member of the community founded by John
Date: A.D. 90–100

This thirteen verse Letter begins by claiming that it is being written to a "Lady." In actual fact, the Letter is probably written to a community, not an individual person.

As is the case with so many other Letters, this Letter addresses the false teachings being spread around the community. It encourages people to reject them, particularly those ideas which try to "modernize" the gospel, those which actually change or destroy it.

Third John

Author: See Second John
Date: See Second John

This tiny, fifteen verse Letter is a real jolt to anyone who thinks the early Church was free of politics and power struggles.

Jude

Author: Uncertain
Date: About A.D. 90

The author of this Letter attempts to counteract the influence of a bunch of first-century Joe Cools who have been going around saying, "Party however and as much as you want — everybody's gonna get to heaven anyway." They've apparently convinced some people that this is the sensible way to look at things.

The author of Jude disagrees — and has some really colorful words for such people.

20

The Book
of Revelation

Author: A man named John; probably neither the John
of the Gospel nor the Letters
Date: About A.D. 90

No, your teacher is not the great beast mentioned in Revelation.
And no, the most recent earthquake wasn't foretold in Revelation
either. And 666 doesn't refer either to Hitler or to a Satanic rock
group.

The Book of Revelation is absolutely the handiest thing to use if
you have an off-the-wall religious idea and you want some proof
for it. With a little imagination you can even prove how the results
of last year's Super Bowl were really destined from all time.

Reading Revelation is an adventure. In one sense, it's the
liveliest of all the New Testament books. There are beasts and
dragons with multiple horns and heads, cosmic battles with stars
crashing down from the sky, and a city made of pure gold.

It's "apocalyptic" writing, a literary form that we do not
regularly use today. In fact, it was really popular only for about two
centuries — the centuries right before and right after Christ. The
Book of Revelation is sometimes called "The Apocalypse," a
Greek word meaning "revelation" or, literally, "uncovering."

This style of writing, to put it mildly, is really different from
anything we're familiar with today. Strange as it may seem, the

wild images of Revelation that confuse us were probably quite clear to the original readers.

On the surface, apocalyptic writing may seem to be a foretelling of future events by means of a vision that contains unexplained symbols.

Sometimes you can understand the symbols if you know a good bit about the history and culture of the times. On the surface, apocalyptic writing speaks of a final, great cosmic battle between the forces of good and evil. Often it includes references to events taking place at the time of its writing. The primary message is certainly intended for the people reading it at that time.

The author calls himself John and writes from a prison island called Patmos (something like Alcatraz used to be). John has been exiled there for being a troublemaking Christian. He knows things are just as bad or worse for Christians in many places throughout the empire. These Christians need encouragement to remain firm in their faith. They need to be told that, in spite of how rotten things look right now, they really are on the winning team.

Read Revelation from beginning to end without being overly concerned about the meaning of any particular verse, reference, or image. Just read it for fun (it is) and to gain a basic familiarity. Then you'll be ready to make some sense out of all the symbolism. Don't expect to understand it all at once. People who have spent years reading Revelation realize that their study will never be finished.

In apocalyptic writing, numbers are symbolic. Four signifies the universe or the world. Six represents incompleteness; so does three-and-a-half. Seven represents completeness and perfection, and is often associated with God. When the Lamb (Jesus Christ) is pictured with seven horns and seven eyes, this is the author's way of saying Jesus has complete power and knowledge. There are seven churches to whom John speaks; but this is his way of stressing that he's talking to the *entire* Church or body of Christian believers.

Twelve stands for Israel. One thousand conveys largeness. A bit of multiplication (12 x 12 x 1,000) gives us 144,000 — which is not the number of tickets God will give out for that Nonstop Feature Presentation in the Sky, or the number of rooms in the heavenly motel. It simply means total fulfillment.

In the prelude to the great battle, the Lamb opens the scrolls by breaking the seals. In other words, history is hidden to everyone but God. Christ, however, has the power to fulfill God's plan for history. Chapter 7 is a preview of the victory scene intended to present the central theme of Revelation, which can be stated simply: No matter what things look like now, God is going to win.

The great battle scenes occur in chapters 8 through 20. Look for the symbols of good and evil. Dragons are obviously bad guys, sometimes standing for evil in general, as in chapter 12, and sometimes specifically for Satan, as in 20:2. The great harlot or whore is John's gross image for Rome, and the scarlet beast she sits upon is the empire itself.

The famous 666 probably refers to the emperor Nero. A numerical table of the alphabet common at that time produces 666 from "Nero Caesar" written in Hebrew. And, whether accidentally or deliberately, we have another symbol: If six represents incompleteness, 666 represents terrible incompleteness — and thus raw evil.

Gog and Magog in chapter 20 symbolize pagan nations. The names themselves are borrowed from the Book of Ezekiel in the Old Testament.

The victory scene in chapters 21 and 22 is gorgeously written. The Church is described as the bride of the Lamb and as the new Jerusalem, now fashioned as an eternal holy city. There's no temple in the city, no place where the presence of God dwells among people, because people themselves now live in the presence of God . . . forever.

That's John's point: "Here's where we're headed. Isn't it terrific? Hang on, remain faithful to Jesus, and we'll get there."

21

And You Have to Read This, Too

The title to this chapter, like the title to the Introduction, is a bit sneaky. This section of a book is usually called "For Further Reading." Some people don't glance at "For Further Reading" sections just as they don't read Introductions. They figure, "I handled *this* book okay, but that 'further' stuff is probably really heavy — I better not try it." Or they might say, "I got confused enough by *this* book — if I do further reading, my brain cells will have a real spasm."

Consider some further reading.

"Further" doesn't have to mean deeper and heavier. Going back over the same territory from a different writer's point of view often brings marvelous results. You can have experiences like those sudden light bulbs they draw above the heads of cartoon characters. There is nothing (well, almost nothing) to match the "Now I get it!" feeling.

There's an absolute mountain of books written about the New Testament in general and the individual books of the New Testament. We could almost make a book by listing all the books.

So we won't.

Instead, let's list types of books that can help you learn about the New Testament. Many of these are books which cover the entire Bible, not just the New Testament.

An *atlas* of the Bible will provide far more than maps. It will contain information on archeological studies and how they affect your understanding of the Bible. You'll find pictures of biblical places as they appear today and pictures of artifacts from biblical times.

A Bible *almanac* is a treasury of factual information. Like modern almanacs, it will give statistics, not interpretations.

A *concordance* is an alphabetical listing of key words in the Bible and all the places (books, chapters, and verses) where these words appear. A comprehensive (practically total) concordance is a huge volume or several volumes.

A *dictionary* of the Bible is an especially valuable tool. A good Bible dictionary will not simply give brief definitions. It will list all or most of the places in the Bible where a concept is found and comment on the varying shades of meaning from one passage to another. Look up "Law," for example, in a Bible dictionary and you should find a column or more of information.

A *commentary* attempts to explain the meaning of the Scriptures. Since the author of a commentary is usually working from a particular religious viewpoint, the interpretation of texts will be different from one commentary to another. If you use a commentary, make sure it's one that's consistent with our Catholic faith.

There are many, many *general introductions* to the New Testament (besides this one). Some concentrate more on interpretation and meaning, others on the cultural or historical background of the New Testament. As I said above, reading more than one is always good business. You will cover some of the same ground (review is good anyway), but it's not likely that a book on something as complex as the New Testament will cover exactly the same things in the same way.

There are many *series* of New Testament studies. Books in the series cover sections of the New Testament (for example, the Gospels) or even individual New Testament books by themselves (the longer ones). These are helpful if you're doing a particular study on one part of the New Testament. A single book on the

Gospel of John, for example, can provide far more background on that Gospel than can be found in a general introduction to the New Testament.

Don't get scared off from further reading. Do some. It's more fun to be involved in sports or similar activities once you know what you're doing and everything isn't a big mystery. It's more fun to read about something — like the New Testament — when you already know a few things about it.